"Having explored and written about lives, Joanne DiMaggio's new book ticks all the boxes for me. The subtitle—"Past Life Clues to Current Life Maladies"—is the basic theme of Joanne's research. However uncovering a past-life connection to a physical or psychological condition in this life is just the first step. The most important aspect of this work is whether it is possible to heal the condition. The twenty-three case studies in the book provide some proof of the therapeutic value of past-life regression and the related karma we bring back with us to resolve in each new life. The case histories in this book provide a valuable insight into the karmic dramas of our 21st-century lives."

—Barry Eaton author of *Afterlife* and *No Goodbyes*

What the participants said about their experience in the physical karma research project:

"It would be nice if medical science and organized religion would be more accepting of past-life experiences and of karmic debt incurred by our past-life actions. It is good that you do such research in these fields. We need more of it."

—Gary

"It [soul writing] allows us to consciously connect with spirit and receive guidance with our eyes wide open in this world in this lifetime, which helps to bring us back to the present moment. Writing is a way to heal!"

—Louise

"You have given me a part of my life, heart, and soul back through these sessions. It was supposed to be my year of self-care and love and this has only helped that."

—Anila

"The issues with my parents don't seem so bad anymore and I have less fear over my survival because I saw what I faced in that past lifetime."

—Jack

"I believe that recognizing the root cause can help you begin to alleviate your health problems. I have a different mindset on how I am approaching my life. Simplifying my life will change how I feel every day. This is such a valuable lesson that I could not clearly see until my regression. I will always be grateful."

—Janet

"I am so very grateful that I was able to experience this past-life regression session. Being open-minded and learning more about alternative explanations allows for me personally to be more accepting of my condition and my current life rather than turning to anger and resentment for ways of dealing with my pain and mental state. I thank you very much for your time and your expertise in this line of work."

—Joan

"The regression and the follow-up work is a transformative process that continues to unfold."

—Kathie

*Dedicated to the
living legacy of
Edgar Cayce*

Books by Joanne DiMaggio

Soul Writing: Conversing With Your Higher Self

Your Soul Remembers:
Accessing Your Past Lives through Soul Writing

KARMA
can be a real
PAIN

Past Life Clues to
Current Life Maladies

JOANNE DiMAGGIO

RAINBOW RIDGE
BOOKS

Cover and interior design by Frame25 Productions
Cover photo © CHOATphotographer c/o Shutterstock.com

Edgar Cayce Readings © 1971, 1993-2007
by the Edgar Cayce Foundation
All Rights Reserved.

Published by:
Rainbow Ridge Books, LLC
140 Rainbow Ridge Road
Faber, Virginia 22938
www.rainbowridgebooks.com
434-361-1723

If you are unable to order this book from your local
bookseller, you may order directly from the distributor.

Square One Publishers, Inc.
115 Herricks Road
Garden City Park, NY 11040
Phone: (516) 535-2010
Fax: (516) 535-2014
Toll-free: 877-900-BOOK

Visit the author at:
www.joannedimaggio.com

Library of Congress Cataloging-in-Publication Data applied for.

ISBN 978-1-937907-45-7

10 9 8 7 6 5 4 3 2 1

Printed on acid-free recycled paper in the United States of America

Acknowledgements

This book would not be possible without the fifty men and women who volunteered to be a part of my yearlong research project. While I could not share all of their past-life experiences and discoveries, each of them nonetheless played a significant role and I am grateful for their willingness to embark on this fascinating journey with me.

My thanks to author P.M.H. Atwater for her thought-provoking insights and input on the first draft, as well her urging that I find and express my voice. She is a most wise mentor, an admired colleague, and a dear friend.

I am indebted to Karen Davis at the Edgar Cayce Foundation, not only for the time she spent reviewing the Cayce readings in this book for accuracy, but also for her constant support, loving advice, and soul-lifting encouragement. It is always a joy to work with her.

I'd also like to acknowledge Dr. C. Norman Shealy, whose opening remarks at a Medical Intuition Conference in Virginia Beach, in which he expressed his belief that there was a connection between illness and past lives, unknowingly flipped on the "idea" light bulb that culminated in this book.

But most importantly, I am grateful to Edgar Cayce, whose enduring legacy remains the cornerstone upon which this eager student continues to pursue her soul's work.

—Joanne DiMaggio, MA, CHt
June 2016

"Hold the presses . . . *nobody is approaching reincarnation and past-life hypnotic regressions like Joanne DiMaggio*. She tackled the claim that 'all disease or illness is past-life related,' invited in dozens and dozens of people with non-responsive physical ailments, then explored possible causative factors through hypnotic regressions. Yup, all cases pointed to unfinished business in past lives. What's really exciting, though, is that she invited clients afterward to ask their soul to comment about the session. Joanne did the same thing too. Utilizing both sources, helpful information emerged that led to healings. Her first book, *Soul Writing*, revealed that anyone can do this, allow their own soul to express itself via a meditative state and to write down thoughts or feelings that might be helpful. *Karma Can Be a Real Pain* is a surprise."

—P. M. H. Atwater, L.H.D., researcher of near-death states and spiritual transformations, author of *Dying to Know You: Proof of God in the Near-Death Experience*

Contents

Introduction

When I was in college, one of my history professors called me into his office to discuss a paper I had written. He was an intimidating sort and I was terrified of him, so to be summoned to his office filled me with dread. I timidly sat across the desk from him, quietly fidgeting in my chair as he intently stared at me. After what seemed like hours, he said, "Joanne, you have the most uncanny feel for the 18th century of any student I've ever had." I smiled with relief. I knew it was true, even though at this point in my life, I did not attribute that "uncanny feel" to reincarnation. Yes, I read books about reincarnation throughout my teens, and yes, there were a number of clues from my childhood as to why I responded to 18th century American history as if I had lived it, but I never put two and two together.

Curious about why I felt such a kinship to this time period, after graduation I convinced a friend to join me in visiting historic locales from Virginia to Massachusetts. My hope was that one of them would reveal the secret behind my unexplained attraction to early American history.

I didn't have to wait long to get an answer. Just a few days into the Virginia leg of our trip, I began experiencing heart palpitations and shortness of breath, accompanied by a strong sense of déjà vu. It was very bizarre and I could not explain it except to think maybe it was something I ate. Luckily, that sensation did not manifest elsewhere on our journey and I filed it away in that part of my brain where I stored inexplicable experiences. A few years later, I married and began raising a family in suburban Chicago, living what I thought was a rather conventional existence.

That all changed after *Out on a Limb*, a television mini-series based on Shirley MacLaine's groundbreaking book, aired in January 1987. Its strong emphasis on reincarnation relit my previous curiosity about past lives, so I got involved with Edgar Cayce's Association for Research and Enlightenment (A.R.E.) and the now disbanded Association for Past Life Research and Therapies (A.P.R.T.).

Over the next few years I ardently pursued the study of every aspect of reincarnation. This exploration eventually uncovered information that gave me a plausible explanation as to why I felt such a kinship to 18th century Virginia, but more importantly, gave a reason why issues I was dealing with in the here and now were linked to a previous lifetime.

In an effort to learn more, I returned to Virginia in 1993 and retraced my steps where I had had that strong physical response some twenty-two years earlier. This time my reaction was much more debilitating than mere déjà vu, as I felt a sharp burning sensation in my lower spine. The pain was excruciating and I could barely function.

Somehow I got on a plane and returned home where I sought relief from a number of doctors, including my primary care physician and several chiropractors—all to no avail. X-Rays showed nothing. Pain meds did nothing. Exercise gave no relief. For six months, absolutely nothing worked. Finally, out of desperation, I consulted with David Roell, a gifted channeler who was able to read my Akashic Record.

The Akashic Records are the equivalent of the Universe's super computer, containing every thought, word, and deed attributed to our soul since creation. Think of it as a big library in the sky with a book that contains your soul's biography. While some Akashic readers would have you believe only they can find and read your Book of Life, as Edgar Cayce called it, the truth is, through guided meditation, you can do this as well. I hadn't learned how to do that yet, so I asked David to do it for me. Knowing I had first experienced this pain while visiting an 18th century locale, I reasoned that if it were past-life related, it had to do with that lifetime. Sure enough, it did. David's channel told me that the reason I was feeling that pain was because in that life, I had been hit in the back with a fireplace poker in the very place where I first felt the pain. This later was confirmed by Betty Riley, another gifted intuitive I knew through the A.R.E. Without telling her what David revealed, she nonetheless shared the very same explanation.

Soon after the source of that pain was revealed, it disappeared. Learning the origin of the pain, it was no wonder I felt that "burning" sensation—and not surprising that traditional medical intervention failed to release that pain the way the truth of its origin did.

While I never forgot that incident, I nonetheless did not think about it in the context of physical karma. That's because when it occurred in 1993, I was not yet a past-life therapist, so case studies involving physical karma were not in the forefront of my mind. I was, however, passionate about past-life research and by then had formed my own past-life organization, called PLEXUS (Past Life

Exploration, Understanding and Sharing). Through PLEXUS, and through the A.R.E., I met many professionals involved in reincarnation studies. They became my mentors.

Upon disclosing the facts about my own past-life journey, the late Henry Bolduc, an A.R.E. author and lecturer who was considered an expert on reincarnation, said I knew more about reincarnation than most past-life therapists, so why wasn't I doing past-life work myself? I was flattered at the compliment, but adamant that I didn't want to be a therapist. I was a writer and saw my role as one of observer, researcher and reporter—not as a practitioner. But Henry persisted and eventually, more to appease him than anything else, I became certified as a hypnotherapist and began seeing clients of my own. For this, I say—thank you, Henry!

As a past-life therapist for many years now, I have had a front row seat to the miraculous transformations that occur during a regression session. Each time it happens, I am reminded about how valuable the experience is—not only for the client, but also for anyone else who would read about what ordinary men and women encounter when they explore their previous lifetimes. The magic happens in the office, but the true healing occurs when that magic is shared. And that's what I feel led to do more than anything else.

So now, why this book? I always have paid attention to synchronistic events, or as Carl Jung called them—"meaningful coincidences." A few years ago, I noticed a shift in my regression practice. Suddenly I was getting requests for sessions from individuals who suspected that their present life ailments were rooted in a previous life. These were people suffering from all manner of chronic conditions. They had sought relief through traditional means but came up empty handed. The condition persisted.

Somehow, someway, spirit led them to make the connection that their malady may be rooted in a previous life and if so, what better way to confirm this than through a past-life regression?

From my years of doing past-life research, I read many reports suggesting that present-life conditions were the result of karma. It may have been acquired from a mean-spirited attitude toward someone, from an event in which someone did something harmful to another, or vice-versa. Some physical karma came from a wound received in battle; from a last thought as the soul left the body; or even from the manner of death.

As a student of Edgar Cayce, the most renowned psychic of the 20th century and the father of holistic medicine, I began researching hundreds of readings he gave to individuals coming to him with physical complaints—everything from acne to venereal disease. Fortunately, some of these lucky souls also had a life reading, for it is in the life readings that Cayce's Source explained why their present-life condition was the result of actions they took in a previous life.

Adding to this, I often heard my colleagues talk about spontaneous healings that occurred as a result of a past-life regression. When a client uncovered the source of their physical malady, coupled with a greater connection to spirit, it led to healing—as if spirit was saying, "Well, now you know WHY you are dealing with this today, but it's over and done with. You don't need the reminder anymore so therefore, you don't need this condition anymore" and it was gone.

My skeptical side thought this was not possible—that there must be another explanation. I cringed when I thought of how the medical community would react to such a statement. Yet the part of me that believes nothing is impossible in this universe embraced the idea of spontaneous healing as a true possibility. After all, I only had to look at my own experience to know that.

And then, as if to confirm this fact, I was privileged to see it happen to one of my own clients during the research I conducted for my second book, *Your Soul Remembers: Accessing Your Past Lives Through Soul Writing.* In his case, death by suffocation in Pompeii came back to manifest as asthma in this life as a reminder to not repeat the behavior patterns of the past that led to his death. Since I always add a soul-writing session to the end of each regression, he was able to answer the question I posed, which was: "Ask your soul if there is anything more about that life that was not revealed in the regression." The first sentence he wrote was a question, "Asthma the result of seared lungs?" That was his ah-ha moment. He reported that the asthma disappeared soon thereafter. It had done its job and was no longer needed.

This was typical of the volunteers who came to this project and pointed to an underlying truth about dealing with physical karma. In "Inner Healing from Past Lives," an article in the September/October 2004 issue of A.R.E.'s magazine, *Venture Inward*, George Schwimmer wrote, ". . . a physical symptom is, indeed, a message about a core issue/lesson. The pain and the past-life wounds (physical, mental, emotional, electromagnetic) must ultimately be healed, of course; but the core issue/lesson must also be found, examined and dealt with in a positive, healing way."

In "Healing Effects of Past-Life Regression," published in the April-June 2010 issue of *Venture Inward*, Gregg Unterberger wrote: "For the regression to be healing involves not only understanding the roots of a negative pattern or recurrent issue—which often arches over many lifetimes—but may include an emotional release so that the clarity can be fully internalized."

Shortly after my second book was published, I began getting the message in my meditations and in counseling from gifted intuitive readers that I should look into how I could incorporate medical intuition into my regression practice. This led me to a conference sponsored by the A.R.E. on Medical Intuition. It featured C. Norman Shealy, M.D., PhD, one of the world's leading experts in holistic medicine, and Caroline Myss, a medical intuitive who became a *New York Times* bestselling author, lecturer, and mystic.

When Dr. Shealy first started speaking, I was astonished to hear him say that all disease or illness was past-life related. It was a bold statement, to be sure, and I wasn't certain I heard him right. However, some time later I read a statement he posted on his website that confirmed my ears had not deceived me. He wrote, "In my experience all significant illnesses/accidents, etc. in this life are the result of unfinished business from a previous life. Anger, guilt, anxiety and depression often are triggered by an event in this life which triggers the subconscious memory left over from a similar event in a past life."

He wasn't the only respected physician who made such a claim. Dr. William A. McGarey, former Medical Director of the A.R.E. Clinic and Director of the Medical Research Division of the Edgar Cayce Foundation, said: "I've come to the conclusion that most of the serious, long-term, degenerative diseases are karmic in their nature."

When I decided that physical karma would be the topic for this book, I thought about how to create a research project that would include case histories to prove that the subject's current physical condition was indeed the manifestation of karma acquired in a prior lifetime. To do this, the project was divided into three parts. The first involved a screening process of interested volunteers. This was done via a qualifying questionnaire asking about their chronic condition and why they felt they were a good fit for the project. Those who qualified came to my office for a consultation, followed by a past-life regression and soul-writing session.

Each session began with a deep relaxation exercise in which we focused on every part of their body—from their toes to their scalp. As we examined each part, I asked them to do a scan and tell me if they were experiencing any discomfort or sensitivity in that part of their body.

Michael Talbot, author of *Your Past Lives, A Reincarnation Handbook*, writes about using resonance to identify body karma. To do this, he suggests individuals interested in determining whether they are experiencing body karma should focus on the body part, paying attention to areas that have given them repeated problems.

"Unusual sensitivities about certain parts of your body can also indicate body karma," he wrote. "An aversion to things pointed to your eyes or head may indicate a latent past-life memory of a head injury. If you are especially sensitive about wearing scarves or items of clothing which fit snugly around your neck, you may have suffered a neck injury in a previous life. Even something as simple as a slight nervousness or over-protectiveness about a certain part of your body may be a clue that will allow you to unlock a past-life memory."

In my study, I found that sensitivities that came up in a body scan often previewed what was to come in the regression, as if spirit was already at work alerting the participant that a past-life trauma occurred in that part of their body.

The question about birthmarks grew out of the work of Dr. Ian Stevenson, whose research unearthed evidence that suggested that physical, as well as emotional conditions, could be transferred from one lifetime to another. His landmark work with children drew special attention to birthmarks. He outlined his findings in "Birthmarks and Birth Defects Corresponding to Wounds on Deceased Persons," a paper he presented at the Eleventh Annual Meeting of the Society for Scientific Exploration held at Princeton University, June 11-13, 1992, and published the following year in *The Journal of Scientific Exploration*. The paper presented evidence that physical characteristics, such as birthmarks and deformities, may be carried over from a past life to a present life.

In my work, once the scan was complete and the participant was in a deep state of relaxation, I proceeded with the past-life regression, leading them to what appeared to be an endless hallway in an old, historic hotel. The hallway had doors on each side, just as it would in any hotel, but instead of each door displaying a room number, it had a year on it, starting with the year of their birth in this life on the door closest to them. The next door had the year of their most previous past life, and subsequent doors had the years of the lives before that, going all the way back in time to when their soul first inhabited a physical body. They were instructed to walk down the hallway and to allow their soul to stop them in front of the door leading to the past life that was the origin of their current physical condition. Behind that door was a living representation of that past life, as if they were walking on to a movie set that was filming a period piece—except this film was about them.

Once we were in the past-life room, the regression began with the traditional identifying questions, such as what they looked like, what they were wearing, their age, sex, etc. The middle portion of the regression asked their soul to scan that life and find a major event or turning point that was so significant it made an imprint on their soul and they brought it with them into this life to complete its karmic lesson.

Once that had been explored to their satisfaction, we moved to their death in that life. I asked what were their last thoughts as their soul left their body, as at that moment they often got insights they had not experienced before. Roger Woolger, a psychologist, lecturer and author specializing in past-life regression, writes that, "consciousness is at the highest degree of intensity at death, with the result that thoughts and feelings that occur in this transition are deeply imprinted on the transmigrating consciousness."

Case in point. A young woman came to my office wanting to know the origin of the psoriasis that covered nearly every part of her body. In the regression, I asked her soul to show her what precipitated this condition. She went back to a life in which she was a prostitute in the old West. When I asked what were her last thoughts at death, she replied that she did not want to be touched. Since this was an obvious commentary about her former profession, one might   assume her karma in this life would focus on her sexuality. Instead, her karma was quite literal. She put it out to the Universe that she did not want to be touched, so she came back and manifested a skin condition that kept people at a distance. That's how karma works. Obviously, the Universe was listening to her request!

Many of the last thoughts of my volunteers reflected the despair they experienced in the lifetime they revisited. Francine, who willed herself to die after losing her fiancé, thought: "What's the use? I'll never be happy." Jack, who was crucified, died thinking: "I could trust nobody." And Meg, who died of a drug overdose, said her last thoughts were: "My life was worthless." These thoughts planted seeds that bloomed in their current life, so in examining them, we were given powerful clues as to the origin of the karmic issues they were dealing with in the here and now.

After the death scene, I asked a series of final questions to finish the session. The first asked the client to study the parallels between their previous and current lives, looking for similar behavior patterns, attitudes or situations. Then I asked them to focus on the individuals in their previous life and to get in touch with the essence of their souls to see if the same energy existed in someone in their current life—reminding them that we change sexes and relationships in each life, but we nonetheless travel as soul families from one life to the other. If they identified the soul from a past life in the body of someone in their current life, I asked them to reflect on what role those souls were playing now. That concluded the regression portion of the session.

One could argue that the work outlined thus far is hardly groundbreaking and I would be the first to agree, for many respected and renowned past-life specialists have written on this topic before. What sets my study apart, however, is the inclusion of soul writing. At the end of each regression, I put a pad of paper on their lap and a pen in their hand and instructed each participant to ask their soul to provide any additional information it could to explain, clarify or provide the backstory about that lifetime that did not come through the regression. As they wrote, I also did my own soul writing, asking my Source to provide information I could share with them.

Soul writing, based on the Edgar Cayce readings on inspirational writing, is a written form of meditation. (Instructions on how to do it are in Chapter Ten.) It is writing in a quiet, altered state of consciousness, when an individual is able to set aside their conscious mind and allow their higher mind to connect to a divine Source that provides profound information that is different in tone and context from what they would write in a conscious state. In this heightened state of awareness, they receive answers to questions posed on any topic, including past lives.

George Schwimmer acknowledges that communicating with the higher self gets to the crux of one's issues immediately and confirms how important this connection is to the healing process.

"I've found that talking to the client's higher self is the most critical healing technique," he wrote. "In the space of a few minutes, the higher self can give an overview, along with insights, advice, directions, and sometimes specific ways to deal with specific issues. I'm not exactly certain what the higher self is, particularly as occasionally it refers to itself as 'we' and identifies itself as a group consciousness. However, the higher self usually brings a marked shift in a client's energy, vocal qualities, syntax, attitudes and perceptions, compared to the waking state."

In my practice, I have found soul writing an invaluable tool in supplementing information that came through a regression. Often, this is where the "ah ha" moments happen, as with the man suffering from asthma that I mentioned earlier.

Because soul writing was such a powerful element in this research project, I have chosen to include both the transcript from the regression session and either my soul writing, the volunteer's soul writing or both, to illustrate how the writing was instrumental in helping to integrate the past into the present.

The final part of the project involved a follow-up questionnaire sent to the subject weeks later. The questions were based on their particular experience and were designed to probe deeper, asking whether our uncovering of the past-life incident that set up the physical karma resulted in improving, releasing, maintaining, or worsening their condition. A secondary purpose was to see if, in fact, the soul-writing session provided additional information and guidance for healing.

In all, I conducted nearly 50 regression/soul-writing sessions, using 23 of those in this book. Of these, there were five men and eighteen women ranging in age from 34 to 74 that I worked with from September 2014 through August 2015. My volunteers came from all walks of life, including a professor, a registered nurse, an aerospace project manager, a defense contractor, a flight attendant, a Navy veteran and more. These were all individuals who were well established and respected in their fields—not the sort that would be stereotyped as being prone to imaginary ravings. What is recorded here are examples of ordinary people experiencing extraordinary healing, regardless of whether that healing had to do with their physical body or whether it had to do with their soul. I was hoping it would do both.

I had the privilege of assisting these men and women who explored lives from the 5th century B.C. to the 20th century A.D. They went to Africa, all through Europe, Central America, throughout the Mediterranean, in the Middle East, and of course, in what is now the United States.

As they went on their past-life journey, I went with them, seeing what they saw from a vantage point of a silent, invisible observer who got glimpses of the deeper story that lay beneath the oral history they imparted. This enabled me to ask the questions that led them deeper into the experience and ultimately made the connection between past occurrences and present maladies.

Of course, healing was the ultimate goal of this project, which is why I was so interested in gathering statistics about whether our session had a favorable impact on the chronic condition of each volunteer. Of the twenty-three regressions shared in this book, four individuals experienced a complete healing; seven said their condition improved substantially; eight said their condition was unchanged; two said their condition remained the same, but then got worse; and two could not be classified because they had been healed prior to the regression and had joined the project more to understand the origin of their problem than to heal it.

Mary Ann Woodward, author of *Scars of the Soul: Holistic Healing in the Edgar Cayce Readings,* wrote: "The concept of karma provides a logical explanation for many of our physical ailments and defects. Perhaps we could more readily accept, and would no longer resent, our bodily diseases and imperfections if we understood that these conditions, or 'weaknesses in the flesh,' were self-imposed by the Higher Self so that the soul could learn a needed lesson and thereby free itself of previously committed errors."

Nearly every participant questioned whether he or she made the whole thing up; that it was their over-active imagination that somehow created a story to explain their condition. Roger Woolger addressed this issue in an article in the November/December 1989 *Venture Inward*. "For the therapist there is another kind of truth, psychic truth: that which is real to the patient. As I always tell my clients, 'It doesn't matter whether you believe in reincarnation or not. The unconscious will almost always produce a past-life story when invited in the right way.'"

Emotional reactions to the events in a past life also are indicators of a true experience. Often clients are deeply moved by their recall, some breathlessly sobbing when they relive an especially poignant moment. Or they complain of a physical pain or a shortness of breath in the here and now at the exact moment they experience being injured in the regression or are on their deathbeds succumbing to a respiratory problem.

Getting to the core of that emotional reaction is an essential part of the healing process. Schwimmer wrote, "Clients often came to me with what appeared to be psychosomatic pains, and then discovered that these pains originated from a past life. This indicated that either the past-life damage or the memory of that damage—very emotionally charged—was brought intact into the present-life energy body, which then affected the present-life physical body. In either case, the person was only aware of the physical symptoms."

But make no mistake about it. It is called past-life work for a reason. Karma is work! Past-life therapy takes the client into a much deeper level of exploration where powerful emotions and sometimes disturbing memories rise to the surface. As such it is not a source of entertainment, nor is it fodder for parlor games at a dinner party. This is profound, psychological work that a practitioner cannot learn to do in a weekend certification course. It is serious work best left in the hands of individuals who have the credentials and experience to guide a soul into these sacred inner realms.

There is much you can learn from the past to enable your present. Past-life regression guides you to the previous life most impacting you now so you can see the long-buried feelings, behavior patterns, attitudes and recognize the souls who were prominent in your past and have returned with you in this life to play a pivotal role in your soul's growth. Thus, physical karma obtained in a previous life can be uncovered and healed, often in just one session.

But what *is* physical karma? Mary Ann Woodward defines it as "a manifestation of karmic law taking place at a visible or physical level within the human body."

Harold J. Reilly, Ph.D. (1895-1987) was a world-renowned physiotherapist and a pioneer in the field of massage. He owned and operated the famed Reilly Institute in New York City for more than 30 years. Reilly was a close friend of Edgar Cayce and worked with the Cayce remedies throughout his career.

Addressing the topic of physical karma, Dr. Reilly said:

> " . . . if a man continues to dissipate for an entire life, without taking corrective measures, you would not expect, would you, to see him emerging in another life with a brand-new body perfect in all parts and functioning as if it had never been misused? Then if you believe in reincarnation with its law of karma— an eye for an eye and a tooth for a tooth, as you sow so shall you reap—you must include the body in that plan." (*The Searchlight*, "Healing Begins in the Mind," Vol. 12, No. 2, February 1960).

Woolger says that past-life memories become embedded in the subtle body, defined as layers of energy that surround and penetrate the physical body. Writing in *Healing Your Past Lives, Exploring the Many Lives of the Soul,* he said: "Both past-life research and past-life therapy have now collected an impressive array of evidence to show that these old traumas, inherited through the first level of the subtle body . . . consistently re-imprint in the living body as rashes, deformities, birthmarks, weaknesses in certain limbs, or organic disorders such as a weak bladder, a weak heart, gynecological problems, and so on."

It is important for subjects not to just look at events as they happened either to them or by them, but also to dig a little deeper and explore their attitudes as well. Woodward writes: "For our attitudes and emotions, our resentments, our lives and hates may have persisted from a previous incarnation, causing psychological or psychosomatic problems which finally culminate in some serious illness or accident, or at least perpetuate an imaginary ailment."

Examining attitudes from a previous life takes some introspective work. Once you make the connection, the healing takes place. Uncovering origins, seeing how they have come back to remind us to resolve the negative behavioral patterns that led to the physical condition in the first place, is an important part of the healing process.

As Woodward puts it: "Since we bring the condition or problem with us when we are born, the spiritual errors of former lives lead the soul to choose a new body which will be genetically weak in these areas in which the soul needs to acquire a lesson."

A fascinating aspect of past-life work is to look at cases in which the physical karma of the individual was meant more as a lesson to the parents and others who had a close relationship with him or her. Often highly evolved souls "volunteer" to come into a physical body that is challenged in some way, not so much because of their karmic debt, but more about how their condition impacts those around them. Health challenges that we would consider a burden are actually the result of a selfless choice on the part of the soul. They agree to come in with this condition, knowing it will provide soul growth opportunities for others. It isn't so much what has befallen them that is the issue, but rather how those around them react and respond to them. As a bonus, it accelerates the growth of the soul who agreed to experience the condition.

Michael Newton, PhD, author of *Journey of Souls, Case Studies of Life Between Lives,* writes: "As souls we choose our bodies for a reason. Living in a damaged body does not necessarily have to involve a karmic debt we are paying off because of past-life responsibility for an injury to someone else . . . this choice can involve a learning path to another type of lesson."

Understanding the past-life origin of a physical condition in this life is one thing. Healing is quite another. Can chronic conditions heal after a past-life regression? Absolutely. Just ask those in my study whose condition improved substantially after discovering its origin. But does that work for everyone? Can we reverse or heal deep-seated physical karma, including psychological or psychosomatic diseases that manifest physically? The answer to that question depends on the individual—how he or she responds to the information they uncover; whether they make the necessary changes on the mental and spiritual level; and where the condition had its origins; to manifest a permanent healing. There are no shortcuts here—not ways to circumvent the past to avoid dealing with it in the present or the future. Here is where the individual comes face-to-face with their past, accepts responsibility for seeing karmic patterns and more importantly, works through them.

Sylvia Cranson and Carey Williams, writing in *Reincarnation: A New Horizon in Science, Religion and Society*, stated: "Must we wait for ages to bring harmony and healing into our lives? Would it not help right now to realize there is a wholeness within that is never sick, that can be our base for healing? [Marilyn] Ferguson quotes an anatomist: 'The healer inside us is the wisest, most complex, integrated entity in the universe.' It became so wise, perhaps, because it is the efflorescence of numerous lives of experience. If so, 'there is always a doctor in the house.'"

But it is Garrett Oppenheim who summed it up best in his article, "A Karmic Case of Polio" in the November/December 1989 issue of *Venture Inward*: "I have come to look on my handicap as a gift, enabling me to understand the afflictions of others, to enlarge my horizons and to become, I hope, a better person."

The following chapters illustrate how ordinary men and women met their past-life aspects and came to terms with what occurred in the past, resulting in a healthier, happier life in the here and now—and beyond.

Yes, karma can be a real pain, but lucky for us, there is a cure!

Chapter One

Arthritis and Joint Disease

"Count each affliction, whether light or grave,
God's messenger sent down to thee."
— Aubrey Thomas DeVere: Sorrow

According to the Arthritis Foundation, over 50 million Americans have arthritis, making it the number one cause of disability in the country. Despite how common it is, the Arthritis Foundation admits it is a disease that is "not well understood." If it is not well understood among traditional healers, imagine their reaction when adding the metaphysical component to it. Yet ironically, it is the karmic approach to this crippling disease that makes perfect sense.

One of the underlying reasons for an individual to suffer the pain and joint mutilation brought about by this disease is rooted in their attitude. Some of my arthritic clients admit to being rigid in their thinking, unable to show any flexibility when confronted by someone or something that challenges their beliefs. The tightness they hold in their attitude toward life is reflected in the tightness that grips their joints. They do not allow their minds to expand and easily move from one viewpoint to another, so it is not surprising that this attitude of immobility manifests as immobility in their physical body as well.

Many of the volunteers who participated in my study came because of the desire to discover the source of their arthritic pain, and those sources were eye-opening for them. Francine's arthritis originated in a life where she was paralyzed from polio; Eve's arthritis came from an early 19th century English lifetime in which her hands were burned; and Gary's arthritis in his thumb joints originated in a Civil War lifetime in which he severed the hands of his opponents with his saber.

I'll Never Be Happy

Francine is a 74-year-old editor who complained of arthritis in her hip and hoped our session would give her a better understanding of why and how the condition originated and the emotional issues that resulted so that she could release it and move beyond its crippling confines.

During our body scan, Francine said it felt as though a needle briefly was pinching her right calf and shin, and she complained of a very slight discomfort in her small intestines. When we got to her head, she could not identify a physical sensation but said strong emotion came up when I mentioned scanning her nervous system. "Something was triggered," she said, adding that she was thinking of her nerve tumors.

Francine regressed to the year 1900 in London, England where she saw herself as a slender woman in her late 20s by the name of Abigail Thomas. Abigail was medium height and had dark brown, slightly wavy hair worn under a bonnet. Her long, heavy-cotton, dark blue dress with a slightly flared skirt covered the tops of her black high-top shoes that were accentuated with laced-up buttons. She was in a city with numerous multi-story residential and business brick buildings on either side of the street.

Her evening meal, consisting of meat, potatoes, and gravy was eaten at home off pewter dishes. Her older sister, Rebecca, whom she described as an attractive woman with brown hair, was at the table.

When Abigail was 30 years of age, she became engaged to a 38-year-old man named Torrance, with whom she was starting a publishing business. When Torrance's name came up, however, Francine immediately went to a scene where she saw herself in his home, as he had had a sudden heart attack and was not expected to live. This realization made Francine weep.

"I can't believe it because I love him so much," she cried. "I can't believe he's leaving me. I keep telling him not to leave me. I'm not even sure that he can hear me. We were going to get married. I'm sitting with him for a little while. Just feels like he's slipping away. I'm very sad. I'm frustrated and angry with him for leaving, but it doesn't feel real—feels like a dream. He was healthy up until then—totally unexpected."

Torrance's death caused Abigail to sink into a deep depression. "I feel like I don't have anything to live for now," she said. "I stop my life. I'm grieving for him. I don't want to live without him."

This despondency goes on for several months. Rebecca tries, but fails, to cheer her sister. Abigail becomes ill soon thereafter and dies six months after Torrance. She had no interest in eating and Francine thought she might have died of a broken heart. More than likely she may have starved herself. Her condition was complicated because she contracted polio, probably while Torrance was still alive, and it crippled her soon after his death. Her last thoughts were, "What's the use? I'll never be happy. The only thing that mattered to me was gone. My life was so totally invested in him. I was feeling pretty helpless and that I'd never see him again."

In comparing Abigail's life to her own, Francine felt the tie-in was "pretty obvious" and that's why her response to the regression was so emotional. Abigail was paralyzed from polio. Francine has issues with pain in her hip and nerve tumors in her body, causing her pain when she walked.

"What I experienced as Abigail was a very emotional issue and probably affected my nervous system," she said. "I think of myself as a fairly emotional person. Plus I have several tumors that wrap around the nerves, which would be equal to a feeling of compression and that could cause pain."

Francine occasionally catches herself having the same negative thoughts as Abigail, adding that she was raised in a victim conscious environment.

"Thinking victim thoughts can become a self-fulfilling prophecy," she said. As an adult, she realized thoughts were powerful and thinking victim thoughts can become a self-fulfilling prophecy. Consequently, she was working hard to overcome negative thought patterns, but admitted they still materialized from time to time.

Like Abigail, Francine has not married in this lifetime. While she has fallen in love many times, it usually was one-sided, which would mirror the one-sided love Abigail felt for Torrance after his death.

Francine is an editor, which picks up the work that Abigail and Torrance wanted to do together. Both Abigail and Francine are romantic souls and both had a tendency to depend on and identify with someone else, especially men.

In terms of people from Abigail's life who are in her life now, Francine identified a man she fell in love with, who could have been Torrance. There was another man she was friends with in this life that she said she could have seen herself with in a relationship. "Last year he did what I did in my last life," she said. "His wife died and he died several years later. If he would have been open to it, we could have had a relationship, but he was too focused on his loss."

Francine's Soul Writing

Release. That lifetime is over, gone, done, complete. It taught me so much—too bad it took me so long to learn it. But I chose this lifetime and the ways this waking up/teaching/learning would occur, so everything is perfect. I release my fiancé from that lifetime, all anger and sadness I felt with him and about him and I now start a brand new life, with a much lighter load. Now I can truly enjoy life and I am so grateful for this major learning and release. I am love. I am light. I need no one else to define me. I am an expression of the divine. I now move forward joyfully, one foot in front of the other, pain free, karma free, to do the work I came to do, to be peace, to spread peace, to bring peace to those around me. Now I can open up my heart and life to that special soul mate I have been searching for all this lifetime. I know that he will reveal himself to me very soon because he has been searching for me as well. Together we will do our soul work. I am healed. I am healed. I am healed. And so it is!!

In our follow-up, I shared with Francine that I considered the repetition of the phrase, "I can't believe," as significant and wondered if she had any insights into why that came up so often.

"It may indicate an unwillingness to accept what is so and/or a feeling that I didn't deserve what I got," she replied.

In her body scan, when I mentioned the nervous system, something was triggered within Francine that led her to think about her tumors. I wondered if there was something else that caused that reaction and asked why she thought the phrase "nervous system" served as a trigger point. She didn't know, but added only that, "there is a sadness deep inside of me and I sometimes wonder if, for whatever reason, I am more emotionally vulnerable than the average person."

Abigail's last thoughts were: "What's the use? I'll never be happy." Knowing that last thoughts often set up the next lifetime, I asked Francine if those sentiments have impacted her in this life.

"I do have a tendency to notice what's missing or to think, 'If I had such and such, I could be happy.' However, at the same time I feel blessed and extremely grateful for the abundance I experience every day of my life."

In reviewing Francine's regression, I suggested that her fiancé's early death may have been pre-arranged in spirit as a way to give her the opportunity to learn self-love and to pull on the strength she had to move forward. I speculated that had she done that, the polio might not have been necessary. I asked if she had learned the lesson of self-love and she said she had.

"I have learned a lot about self-love in this lifetime and the lesson continues," she said. "Also I have had to be self-sufficient and self-reliant in this life, so although I don't always feel strong, a review of my life experiences reveals that I have had the strength to move forward when it was necessary, and I believe that will continue."

I speculated that the arthritis in her hip in this life not only may be a remnant of her short bout with polio, but also was symbolic of not being able to move forward—of remaining stationary or stuck in her emotional body. Francine agreed with that assessment, adding that in this life she, too, was stuck in an emotional impasse and her arthritis was symbolic of her unwillingness or reluctance to move ahead.

The regression, therefore, revealed two issues: self-love rather than outside validation; and, second, moving forward effortlessly with no obstacles or barriers. I asked Francine to reflect on how this has manifested in her life and if she felt those issues have been or will be resolved.

"I think this lifetime has been very much about both of these issues," she said, "and I have made a great deal of progress. The physical challenge I am dealing with now (arthritic hip and possible surgery) will definitely accelerate the resolution of these issues."

Francine exhibited some resistance in the regression, the result of not wanting to relive the traumatic experience of Abigail's life. Consequently, she would not allow herself to surrender to the experience and go in very deep. Nonetheless, she got what she needed.

"Some of the information was not new to me, but the polio piece was new, and this brought up a lot of emotion as well as understanding," she said. "It was the missing piece that tied everything together."

Francine reported a sense of release at the end of the regression, which made her soul-writing experience all the more meaningful. "The soul writing helped me to realize how much the experiences of that lifetime have been impacting this lifetime and holding me back," she said. "It also helped me to declare that lifetime complete, finished, done, so that I can now move forward."

Francine said her condition remained the same, if not a little worse, after the session and subsequently underwent hip replacement surgery. Acknowledging that healing comes on many different levels, Francine added that while she declared herself healed in her soul writing and that she does believe she was healed at some level, "healing is often a process. It may not occur in an instant, and although I would much prefer to be healed energetically and spontaneously, sometimes it is necessary to enlist the help of skillfully trained medical professionals, whom we are indeed fortunate to have so available."

The Price I Had To Pay

Eve is a 59-year-old retired project manager in the aerospace industry who never had a past-life regression before. She came to the project complaining of chronic arthritis in her hand.

Some months before volunteering for my project, she went on a retreat during which the group extensively explored karma, piquing her interest in her own karmic history.

Eve's body scan revealed a throbbing ache in her left big toe and ball of her foot. There was a tingling in her left arch and heel. She described her left foot as feeling tingly with a little numbness, as if it were in fizzy water. She felt coolness in her left knee and some discomfort in her right hip area. Her sacral chakra was spinning and she felt a gentle throbbing in the center of her chest. She identified moles on her right leg, three in her lower abdominal area, in her lower back, one below her right shoulder, and one on the left side between her breasts. There was some tingling in her left hand mostly centered on the thumb and base of thumb. She felt a twinge above and below her left elbow, and coolness inside the elbow. She reported a throbbing pain in her right shoulder and said both shoulders felt tight with slight tingling in her right shoulder.

Eve went back to a life in 1838 in Yorkshire, England. She saw herself as a wiry, short, slender 15-year-old girl by the name of Bethany Miller. She had tangled, shoulder-length dirty brown hair that had a little curl to it, and she wore a kerchief on her head. She was dressed in a colored top over a skirt made of a rough cream-color material. Her brown, cloth shoes were dusty. She had an abundance of freckles and her arms were browned from the sun.

Her surroundings consisted of rolling hills that were golden, like wheat. She saw a cluster of small buildings, including a farmhouse. A fence marked the boundary around the property, and she could see trees in the distance. There were low buildings made of stucco with thatched roofs and reed fences. One building was a blacksmith shop, with an anvil and various metal farm tools inside. A small, windowless house used a leather cloth for a door opening. There was a small fireplace inside. There also was a shack, a shelter for the pig, and a dirt path between the buildings. A dog and some chickens were running around the yard.

Bethany took her evening meal alone, sitting at a rough wooden table, lit by a candle, in front of a fire. She ate bread and cheese with her hands from a metal plate. Her significant event occurred on a rainy day when she was 18.

"I'm in the house," she said. "Someone is coming into the house, a male stranger. He was looking for my uncle who is a blacksmith. I tell him he's not there but is coming back soon. I offer to give him something to drink. He grabs me and I push him away and he hits me and I fall. I keep getting something about my hand going into the fire."

Injuring her hand in the fire scared off the intruder and he left. She dipped a cloth in water and wrapped it around her throbbing hand and then left the house, barefoot, in search of help. There were children nearby, but they were scattered in the half-dozen other cottages on the property. A little boy named Nathan took her to his house. His mother put fat on her hand and rewrapped it more securely. She put a blanket around Bethany, sat her in a chair and brought her something hot to drink. She then sent Nathan to find Bethany's uncle, who was working on another farm.

"He is like a father to me," she said of her uncle, adding that her parents were deceased. When Bethany tells Nathan's mother what happened, the older woman shakes her head and chastises Bethany, saying if she had married a local boy named Peter, this wouldn't have happened. Bethany's response is: "He's stupid. I couldn't marry him."

When it grows dark, Bethany returns home and finds her uncle there. He comforts her, telling her everything will be okay. "I'm more upset because I can't work around the house and care for the chickens but he is telling me not to worry," she says.

After some weeks have passed, she finds her uncle at home, smoking a pipe and reading something, which she finds strange.

"I didn't think we had anything to read or he knew how to read," she says. "Maybe it's a letter. Somehow I feel it's going to change my life."

She was right. Her uncle had procured a job for her in a distant town. It took her two days to get there and she was amazed at how big the town was. With that letter in her pocket, she began searching for the right house. Seeing so many streets confused her, but she eventually found it. She was being employed in the kitchen of that home, adding that while her hand bore scars from the accident, by this time it was much better.

Her employers had small children she described as "nice" and said the wife taught her to read. After she was there for a few years, she met a young deliveryman by the name of Sim, short for Simpson, and the two marry. Sim is experienced at caring for horses, so he gives up his delivery job and joins Bethany as a stable hand at the family's country home. Ten years later, Bethany and Sim have their own cottage and some land, given to them by their employers.

Bethany dies in her little house, surrounded by her surviving children and grandchildren. She is close to 80 and says she's the last of her peer group to die. "I'm just tired and worn out," she says. Her last thoughts were: "I worked hard all my life and it is just time to rest. I just want to go running in the fields."

Eve felt that Bethany's hand injury was the source of the arthritis in her hand today. "I had a strong pain in that hand the moment I saw the house and fireplace," she said. "I knew I burned my hand before I even went to that incident. I can't explain why I feel certain of this, except perhaps an intuitive knowing in my body. I realized after the body scan that I had omitted a burn scar on the inside wrist of my left hand, just below the area of arthritic pain. According to my mother, I received this accidentally as a child from my father's cigar, though I have no memory of the incident. I definitely would say that this is past-life related to Bethany's burns."

During the regression, Eve said her hand felt heavy. "Feels like it was the price I had to pay to do what I wanted to do—not marry stupid Peter! The price of my happiness. Reminder that happiness doesn't have to come at a price."

In terms of people from that life in her life now, she felt Bethany's uncle was a female friend of hers in this life who makes her feel very peaceful, calmed and healed. Sim is also female and is now her best friend and has given her a place to live. "The man who tried to hurt me seems to be around but I don't want to assume it's someone I'm having difficulty with," she added. "I think Nathan was my best friend's son who died. He was a wonderful boy—died at 13 from a gunshot wound. He was smart and funny."

My Soul Writing

The injury to her hand healed but then, like today, she felt pain and stiffness in it the rest of her life. That pain was a reminder to be cautious and it kept her more alert to what was happening around her at all times—the equivalent of what we'd call "street smart" today. She never forgot the incident but it did not negatively impact her relationship with men, so she was able to enter a happy marriage with Sim. For today, the discomfort in the hand represents the struggle to overcome limitations of any kind—not just physical—and to understand that this can be overcome. It is not so totally debilitating to prevent accomplishing great goals and so serves as a reminder that nothing is an obstacle when approached with love and determination.

Several months after our session, I asked Eve to go back and determine whether she was experiencing any other residual karmic effects today and she said: "It's funny, but I've often felt as though I'd been 'burned' by the men with whom I've had some significant relationships; I've actually used those words. And have definitely developed a reluctance to trust men."

Reviewing the body scan, I asked Eve if she saw any tie-in with Bethany's life experience that would explain those sensitivities and discomforts, starting with the throbbing in her feet. Eve thought it had to do with the fact that Bethany spent most of her early years barefoot in the countryside and her feet were used to walking on rough ground and stones.

When we revisited the discomfort in her right hip she said: "Somehow, I feel this might be related to her later years, after all the hard work on her feet baking."

As for the tingling in her left hand around her thumb; above and below her left elbow, she said: "Again, perhaps from the fire, but also from working hard kneading and baking bread her whole life."

In looking at the parallels between Bethany's life and hers, Eve felt the incident with burning her hand was, "the price I had to pay to do what I wanted to do" but then later added, "Reminder that happiness doesn't have to come at a price." I asked which lesson she took with her in this life.

"I think I connect more with the idea that happiness doesn't have to come at a price," she said. "But perhaps that's just me being optimistic, which is certainly more my outlook in this life. I really have come to believe that it's possible to find joy in just about anything, and that even a bad experience can provide opportunities for happiness."

In her soul writing, Eve wrote that Bethany's neighbors considered her "too bold—like a man—riding horses, starting businesses, but she had no trouble taking care of herself." I asked Eve if she shared those attributes with Bethany.

"I think I have some attributes, such as speaking my mind, doing what I want to do, and taking care of myself," she said. "I worked for 20+ years in a 'man's' profession, as an engineer with Boeing and NASA and was the first woman project manager for a Space Shuttle mission at KSC. I've also got a pretty logical way of perceiving things, and am good at problem solving."

I shared my soul-writing insight with Eve that the discomfort in her hand represented the struggle to overcome limitation of any kind. She said she definitely agreed with that statement.

"Especially in the past few years," she added, "I've taken an approach that love and compassion can bring more results; perhaps I am taking a 'softer' approach to how I accomplish things in my life."

Eve had no prior knowledge of Bethany's life. As this was her first regression, she described the experience as "strange," adding: "At times, I felt as though I were just telling a story, but somehow I knew the experience had happened on some deeper level. It felt right, as though I had actually seen and felt what was happening. Some of the details were so sharp and crisp, and I could see things so vividly. And the emotions I definitely felt on a physical level."

Eve said her condition improved substantially after our session. She acknowledged that our work together reinforced what she always felt to be true, especially in terms of how people in her present life have been around her much longer than she's known them in this lifetime. "It strengthened my belief in the synchronicity of the universe, and how connections are made on a spirit level that we can't explain from simply viewing life as a 'one-shot deal.' From time to time I think about Bethany, and now that I know about her, I sometimes look for links to what is in my life now with her life in the past. It's another interesting perspective in understanding what is going on in my life and with my relationships."

My Brothers In Arms

Gary is a 68-year-old man who spent over 22 years in the U.S. Navy in active duty and 20 years as a defense contractor. He had had a regression before in a group setting and explored several lives, including the one that came up again in our session. He volunteered for this research project complaining of arthritis in both thumbs.

Gary's body scan brought up the memory of a wound in the back of his thigh, as well as wounds above his digestive organs on the right side and a punctured right lung. He recalled injuries to both thumbs and said his right thumb was tingling. His eyes were slightly burning.

Gary's past-life aspect was born in 1832 in Virginia. During the regression he saw himself as a tall, slender 35-year-old man named John. He wore calf-length black boots, a loose white shirt, woolen orange/brown pants, suspenders, a jacket and hat. He had long black straight hair parted down the middle.

The landscape consisted of green rolling hills, an orchard and a split-rail fence. He could see a ranch-style home with a large porch, curtains in the windows, hardwood floor, and a stone fireplace. His evening meal was taken in that same house. It consisted of potatoes, corn and chicken, eaten with silverware off coarse china. Eating with him was his wife Sarah, who had blonde hair that was worn up in a bun, and wore a calico dress. Also at the table were their 6- and 8-year old sons. John was leaving soon to report to his regiment and said he was worried about his family during his absence.

The significant event in John's life occurred during an early Civil War battle. He said he was an officer in the 32nd Virginia Infantry with men under his command. "I'm on horseback," John recalled. "My saber is drawn during a skirmish. I struck the hand of my (Union Cavalry) opponent and severed his thumb. We would fire our pistols first and then we would resort to sabers. I tried to hit the hands of opponents rather than the body [so they] can't ride, hold guns or wield a saber. It happened several times fighting different battles. There were a lot of skirmishes. All I see are the saber fights. I feel a saber cut on my left thigh. It was cared for, treated, and the doctor sewed it up— that hurt worse than the saber cut. Then I went back out there."

A year or so later, he is shot in the chest. He did not recall if he had eye contact with the Union trooper who shot him, as "it happened so fast." He falls off his horse and hurts his back. He was brought to an old log building that was doubling as a hospital. A doctor and orderly cared for him, but six days later he died. When asked what were his feelings about the war, he said, "I wish that it was over, but it was necessary. I was fighting for my home, family and Virginia."

John's last thoughts were concern for his wife and children. He regretted not getting to spend time with Sarah or see their boys grown and married.

Gary indicated that he and John share the same attitude about life—both feeling strongly about what is right or wrong and being willing to go in harm's way for what they believe in.

In terms of people from John's life who are in his life now, Gary said Sarah looked a lot like his present daughter, Lisa. When I asked what role she was playing he said it wasn't to the point of her being a caretaker, but she did express concern for his health and well being and was teaching him patience.

My Soul Writing

John was steadfast in his beliefs and in his desire to defend and protect all that he held dear. His desire was not to kill but to maim—wanting to bring the fighting to an end with the least bloodshed. The arthritis in his thumbs is the result of the actions taken in that life, but he already knew this so nothing new here. He needs to explore John's life prior to this battle to understand his personality more and how his entire being—not just this Civil War experience—is impacting him today. It is much more than just the battlefield experiences that matter. That is only the climax of a life in which other experiences—from childhood onward—made up the man who died on the battlefield. He will find very valuable information if he digs a little deeper to explore that which he has not as yet explored.

In the three months following his session, Gary had no new insights into John's life. I suggested we go a little deeper to discuss what John had said about his feelings toward his family, i.e. that he was worried about their well being in his absence. I asked Gary if that same concern ever came up in this life.

"Concerns for my family in this life, yes," he said. "Each time I left my family for a six month deployment with the Navy,

I would be concerned for my children and my wife who now had to do all that I did. In my past life, the feeling is still there, but then I was concerned for their safety and well being and about their not getting enough to eat. I also was concerned for my wife's safety from Yankee cavalry, as she was attractive and had no man about the house to protect her. We had few neighbors and those we did have were some distance from my farm."

In Gary's case, we see an example of physical karma that is a direct reflection of a past-life act. John drew his saber and struck the hand of his opponent, severing his thumb. In this life, Gary has arthritis in both thumb joints. I asked if he saw the correlation between the two.

"Yes, I do feel that the pain in both my right and left thumb joints are due to my past-life practice of intentionally injuring the thumbs/fingers of my opponents while fighting them with sabers," he admitted. "At present, I have experienced arthritis in no other part of my body, though I am now a 68- year-old disabled veteran. I feel this is a karmic debt I am now facing due to my past life's view of how I would fight, intentionally wounding or disabling opponents with saber strokes aimed at their fingers and hands. Where I could, I would spare their lives but maim them in such a manner. There were many men I did this to. At times the others I rode with in my Cavalry unit did not agree with me as to how I fought. Most of them wanted to kill the Yankee invaders out right with any means available to them."

I asked Gary about how he shares John's attitude of feeling strongly about what is right or wrong and being willing to put yourself in danger for what you believe in.

"In this life I looked forward to adventure and going into harm's way so I joined the Navy and even volunteered to serve as a door gunner in Vietnam," he recalled. "I remember thinking to myself that this was the only war we had at the time and that I didn't want to miss it. Of course, I used the same stupid logic many young men did, that I was bullet proof and nothing bad would happen to me, always to the other guy. Now by comparison with John, I can still feel the anger at the northern states army for invading our state (Virginia) and for disrupting our lives and blockading our harbors. I did not own slaves (most southerners did not, only the larger farms and plantations did). I did not want to leave my wife and two sons at the time, but our militia unit was mustered into active service and I could not go against the needs of my home state so I reported in for duty."

I asked Gary to describe what the regression segment was like for him and he said he felt more relaxed than he had ever been, yet was still aware of lying on my chaise and listening to my voice. "As the memories flooded back into my mind I did feel the emotions/pains/anger of the moments long forgotten but aroused by your questions."

After our session Gary's arthritic condition remained about the same, but he was enthused about the healing potential of past-life regression. "It would be nice if medical science and organized religion would be more accepting of past-life experiences and of karmic debt incurred by our past-life actions," he said. "It is good that you do such research in these fields. We need more of it."

Chapter Two

Foot, Leg and Back Pain

"There are in truth no incurable conditions . . ."
(Edgar Cayce Reading 3744-2).

Let's face it. Who among us hasn't complained about pain in our feet, our legs or our back? I know I have! Karmic conditions in this area of the body quickly emerged as a common theme among many of the volunteers who found their way to my office.

In this chapter we'll explore Emma's past life as a prima ballerina in France where her present day sciatica originated from a career-ending accident she caused for a younger dancer; Ann's past life in 1362 that was the origin of the present weakness in her limbs that she suffers with today; and Christine, whose foot pain stems from a bicycle accident at the turn of the 20th century.

I've Done a Very Bad Thing

Emma is a 65-year-old health care provider who described having sciatica-like symptoms on the left side of her body, especially in her back, hip and leg. This had been a problem for years, sometimes seemingly solved and then resurfacing again after an injury.

She uncovered a great deal of discomfort and sensitivities in her body scan, starting with a wart on the right side of her foot, close to her heel. She felt a sharp pain in her left shin when we started discussing feet, but said it was gone by the time we got to her leg. She described a "sciatica feeling" in her ligaments from the left hip down and as soon as she brought this up, the pain in her shin returned. Her left sacrum was tingling and had pain in mainly her left, but sometimes her right hip. She reported that her solar plexus chakra was partially closed and that something was "off" in her large intestine. On her left side, she described a vibration. "Something to make me notice it," she said. She had a tiny mole beneath her left breast. When we discussed her hands, she said: "In my mind it seems like stigmata, but that makes no sense because there's no mark—it just came to mind." She added that her hands were vibrating and she identified a mole on her left arm. The thoracic area joining the neck was tight. Her right side became uncomfortable as she spoke. She experienced discomfort high up her right shoulder, and in the muscle leading out from her spine to her shoulder tip. She reported that the curvature was "off" in the cervical area of her spine. When we got to her head, she saw a lot of light in the upper part of her skull. "I can hardly see the brain," she said.

Emma went back to a lifetime immediately prior to the French Revolution, describing early events in Paris and later in the French countryside. What was so amazing about Emma's description of this life was that she spoke in a strong French accent, struggling to find the right words in English, much the same way that individuals just learning the language would pause to search for the correct word. Emma later said she had studied French for four years in high school and a year in college. During her second year of high school she "tested off the charts," being able to read French effortlessly.

Emma's penchant for everything French is a clear case of resonance—an experience in which a person is inexplicably drawn to something that makes no sense in the context of this life. Resonance provides very strong past-life clues and exists in all aspects of life if you take the time to look. I use it to help individuals who are wary of hypnosis to flesh out possible past-life aspects. Like detectives, we explore their present-life preferences for art, food, vacation spots, literature, music, books, architecture and yes, language, as left-over attachments from a prior lifetime.

Some past-life therapists have reported clients speaking in the language of their previous life. I had not experienced that in the hundreds of regressions I had conducted, but Emma's uncharacteristic French accent came close and further identified she was having an authentic past-life experience.

So it was that Emma saw herself as Marie Courbienne, a prima ballerina in her 20s. She wore a beautiful costume but was most proud of her pink satin ballet slippers. Marie was short and slender with a tiny, but strong body. She had very long blonde hair that she wrapped around her head when she danced. "I like my hair," she added. "I take good care of it." In her hair was a ribbon, "like a halo of flowers with ribbons coming down, like a costume for a performance."

Marie described being in the middle of Paris on a cloudy, gloomy day. The streets were dirty. She did not like being in the city, saying she preferred living in the country. "I have to be here to dance," she explained, adding she was preparing for an afternoon performance. She stood by a door in a dark alleyway. In the distance she could see horse-drawn carriages.

Marie ate alone in her apartment. Her meal consisted of a plain croissant and some fruit that was brought to her on a plate by her maid. "I have to eat lightly because I perform again [that night]."

When asked about the significant event in that life, she was rather coy. "Oh . . . hmmm . . . . I was very naughty. I tripped someone," she said. "I am scared she take my place. I am jealous. She's very good and I fear her ability so I am causing her to fall and it's done. I've done a very bad thing. I am very sorry. Somehow I put something in the way, like a broomstick. I tried to do it so no one noticed. She's very good in the ballet company and I thought so many times how to do this. Planned it for a while. How mean. I already feel bad, mean, small, and really jealous. Somehow I put it where she tripped. I planned it so no one knows but I know. I know. It is done. She can no longer dance—a break—her upper leg."

Marie said the ballerina in question was nearly five years younger and very beautiful with dark, curly hair. Marie was still in her 20s at this point, but added, "We have short careers and if we are lucky we have a rich man to take care of us and we have a beautiful life."

Marie saw her rival fall, but added that this happened back stage where it was dark. "That's why I can see and implement plan," she said. "She's carried off to doctor. Painful—very. I soon go to light of stage and perform. I am very beautiful but not very beautiful inside to do such a thing. I perform my part. I am prima. I worry she take my place and I no longer prima. She was the only one who could give me competition and I eliminated competition—all gone. I go home to apartment. Carriage waiting to take me there. I have rich, rich silks I put on after performance. I take my little beautiful pink ballet shoes with me. I don't trust them with anyone else. If they were in my shoes it would affect my performance. I go to my beautiful apartment with tall ceilings, big windows, furnishings very plush."

No one ever found out Marie caused the fall and this haunted her for years, causing her to feel shameful in her later years. Nonetheless, it assured her of a long career.

Marie did not keep up with news about the dancer she injured. "In ballet when you're gone, you're gone," she said. "Only present. You fall into non-importance. I hope she had good life. I would feel better if I knew she had a good life filled with love and family." When I asked whether what she did to that dancer was worth it, she answered, "I wonder now that I'm older."

Marie had many suitors but married a nobleman named Jacques with whom she had a long and happy life. She never told him what she did. "I want so much to tell but not want to look bad to him," she explained. "He is kind so I carry the secret, the shame."

Asked about her life after retiring from the ballet, she said: "I live in a beautiful small chateau in the country. I have horses and a stable. We lead a quiet life. No children. I know how fortunate I am." As she talks about her life her mood changes. "Great sadness coming," she says. "I see it ahead."

Marie said the events she described occurred prior to the French Revolution, but that her life of privilege is what led her and Jacques to the guillotine.

"I watch Jacques," she said. "It is the guillotine. People surround us with hate. Jacques first. I am later. I feel so sad. Jacques such a fine man."

Her description of the crowd relayed the volatility of the time. "Angry, angry, angry. Hate, hate, hate crowd. No order. Chaotic. Killing kind people. Jacques very kind. It doesn't make sense to be kind and still guillotine." Her last thoughts were that it was "a beautiful, wasted life."

In considering similarities between both lives, Emma noted that both she and Marie had a childlike laughter, gaiety and exuberance. There was a lot of lightness of being and joy. "The vitality of the body is the same. Same muscular, energetic body." When asked what she thought the physical tie-in was in this life, she said: "Retribution for what Marie did to that girl. Deep shame for what I did."

Emma said in her current life she has a great love of ballet and could always tell if a ballerina was a great dancer. "I knew the hand should do thus and thus," she said, gesturing in a fluid fashion, reminiscent of a ballerina's pose.

Looking at who was in her life then, that is in her life now, Emma identified her daughter as the dancer that Marie had injured. "Rejection, payback. Judgment. She judges me very well. Maybe that is why she rejects me in this life."

Emma's Soul Writing

Bonjour is what you remember so much. It was a time of great growth as you learned from the experience. Yes, your daughter was that girl and your task is to love her all through the rejection. Do not expect love from her, as she must now go on her path. Also through this you fear the future. How will you survive old age with no daughter to support—a daughter in anger? Do not fear for you will be provided for. Your son will be strong support. He is learning the responsibility in his life and will be there. Your lesson is one of love and release of fears. From fear you hurt this girl and your task is to forgive and to give love. You are learning to be love in the highest sense. Your life in present is learning to be love in the present and you are learning to express love and are learning to express as love and are learning to let the ego go as the false construct you know it is. Your task is to give to others and to help others release from ego to be the love you so truly are. You have experienced this path and now will share this knowledge—how to be in spirit love.

Emma had an interesting experience after our session, in that she started thinking in both French and English, which had not happened since her freshman year of college. Her vocabulary was limited, but many words and phrases came through.

In discussing the emergence of the accent during the regression, Emma said it was as if she were two people. "There was Marie trying to describe a life and period in France and also I was observing the whole process," she said. "I could feel her struggling to find the words in English and also struggling to share what it was like for her during this time. I heard what she was saying and could feel her emotions. There was a time when she asked to move forward to the end. There was great sadness and resignation in this request, as she knew what was coming at the end of life. Her subsequent reliving and description of it carried much emotional pain as she had a great, great love for her husband and she was forced to see him guillotined before she met the same fate."

Initially Emma believed her sciatica was retribution for what Marie did to her rival, but as several months had passed since we did the regression, I asked what were her thoughts about the correlation between that event and the physical conditions she was describing now in terms of karmic payback.

"I would not be surprised there was this link," she said. "Oddly enough, although there was this consternation regarding how I could have done such a thing to another human being, I also experienced a feeling of love and acceptance toward Marie. I felt a strange connection to her. Somehow, and I don't understand this, although the act was abhorrent, I felt compassion for her. I still do."

Emma also talked about the relationship with her daughter as that of "rejection and payback" and said she thought she might have been the dancer Marie tripped. I asked if she had given that any more thought and if so, what were her conclusions.

"Our dynamic has been troubled since her teenage years," she said. "I always have thought of her as very special and unique, and of me as courting her approval and never quite reaching this acceptance. She was always her father's girl, and I was never 'good enough' in her estimation. It took my being a counselor at an organization that helped many individuals who struggled with family issues, personality disorders, etc., for me to realize that I had parented her well by comparison. I made mistakes, of course, but always loved her."

Continuing with that theme, I reminded Emma that in her regression she said, "I eliminated competition—all gone." I asked if that was a theme in her present life as well.

"I remember when Marie said that and I thought it odd," she admitted. "She was so matter of fact about it. This was strange because I could feel this detachment as it was discussed. I spoke to someone in this present life who understood the world of ballet and she described a highly competitive situation where the dancer is very insular and completely devoted to her art and the promotion of that art and self as art. She said she would not be surprised that harming another in this way could have happened. In this life, I avoided team sports that were focused on high competitive fervor. Instead, I joined band, swim team, 4-H horseback riding, skiing—mainly competing against my last time or performance. I eliminated competition by pretty much avoiding circumstances that would put me in that kind of a situation."

While Marie may have come across as selfish and self-centered in that lifetime, in her current life, Emma is just the opposite—selfless, kind, and humble, pursuing a career in the healing arts. I asked if she felt she was doing so to make up for what Marie had done.

"I have chosen to work in fields that are in service to others and derive much satisfaction in this," she said. "When I am successful in motivating another to make a change that benefits their long-term health or well being, I light up inside. There is an 'ah ha' moment. It feels right."

It seemed to me that Emma's sciatica was mimicking the condition of the dancer who was hurt so that Emma, unlike Marie, could "feel" what the dancer felt. I asked if she thought that was an accurate statement.

"I had a therapist tell me that I would not confront others because I did not want them to feel the pain I had experienced in my childhood," she explained. "I had to work hard on being able to speak my truth and yet I still avoid confrontation if at all possible. I think the problems in my teenage years, wearing a brace that went from coccyx to armpit, helped me be more aware of others' emotional pain. It helped me, early on, to not feel entitled."

Experiencing the emotions of one's past-life aspect is one indication that the regression experience is real and not fabricated. Emma did this on all levels where Marie's life was concerned.

"When she tried to share with you about where she was living, she touched the drape at the window and I was aware of its heaviness," she said. "I felt her emotions; her great love for her husband; her sense of peace with him in her home; her desire to be away from society and just be quiet and tranquil and nesting with him; her deep appreciation of the beauty of her home and her sense of detachment from others in her ballet troupe. I knew she was not born to wealth and beauty, but ballet brought it to her."

Emma did not know of Marie's life before our session, but added that she suspected she had a past-life history that included ballet because in this life she has a love of ballet and dance. She said she could always pick out whether a performer had the proper hand positions and bodyline.

She said the soul writing helped her understand there was purpose within that life, although she added that hurting another person in that way was not what she could condone or even think of doing now. "Perhaps that life fit into a bigger picture and I was not to pass judgment on Marie," she said. "The soul writing gave me breathing room from the shame of what happened. I still left the session thinking, 'oh my God, how could I have done such a thing?' I felt awful. Later I had to process it and the message from the soul writing helped."

Survival Mode

Ann is a 70-year-old retired Federal Government employee. She came to my project wanting to dig deeper into her hereditary illness, which was weakness in her arms and legs. She was confident it was from a prior lifetime and was seeking increased self-understanding to build on the work she previously did with another past-life therapist.

During her body scan, Ann described her feet as challenged, saying she had a high arch due to muscle loss; weak and swollen ankles and a bone spur on the instep of her right foot. She described muscle loss in her lower legs and at that moment she gave some thought to the use of her lower legs when horseback riding. During this part of the scan, Ann flashed back to a Spanish past life in which she saw herself as a woman scrubbing floors on her hands and knees for a wealthy woman who has incarnated with her in this life. She said weight has always been an issue in this life, admitting she was overly fond of food and had a deep relationship with chocolate.

Ann identified a mole on her middle left-hand finger. She said she had encountered two chronic conditions from prior lifetimes, both affecting her hands and her fingers to the point that she is concerned about safety, typing and picking up things. "I'll have to kill fewer people than I did in the past!" she laughed.

In doing a scan of her spine, she reported muscular soft tissue as being troublesome and said she regularly sees a chiropractor for bodywork and lumbar support. "My bones have always been good," she said, "but I carry tension in shoulder muscles."

She reported discomfort in her left breast. She said her throat bothered her and easily strains if she talks too much. Reflux was something she had been dealing with for five years. She said her neck was getting tense in our session. "It's not as easy to relax as other areas," she said.

Ann's regression took her back to the year 1362. She was a male hunter, soldier, and wanderer named Awf. He was in his 40s, a good size and strong, having done a lot of walking and riding. Awf was tanned, with blue eyes and short, dirty blonde hair that was windblown and unkempt. His legs were bare and he wore makeshift leather sandals. His disheveled, layered clothing resembled old military garb made of a light-colored cloth and very worn dark leather.

Ann had many regressions prior to working with me, but the one as Awf was new to her. She described him as looking off into the distance toward the west where he saw low mountains. The area was mostly barren, filled with rocks and scrub vegetation. There was a bit of a rise looking to the left. "I've been walking some time," she said. "I seem to have some purpose." There were no buildings nearby, but Ann, having taught geography, recognized the area as being near the Caspian Sea, in the Russian steppes. She said many nomadic peoples pass through there.

"I have walked toward the lower mountains and built a fire," she said. "I have my back to the cliffs, looking out. I had been carrying some jerky, eating by hand."

When asked to describe a significant event in Awf's life, Ann relayed information in a stream of consciousness, using isolated words and phrases, yet coherent enough to follow. She said Awf was alone, " because there were wars and my people were killed. I had to move on or be wiped out. I was hurt but not badly. Scattered. Somehow I wound up in this dry distant place. I need to find somebody to stay alive. Wandering a few years. Big battle. Needed to flee. Restless. Many seeking, wanting to find people but not sure I can trust them or they me. Moving away from area that was devastated, slaughtered. Moving from northeast to the southwest. We went across a big swath of Asia. In the beginning we scattered. Some wanted to go in different directions. Some were looking for others. I knew people I loved were dead. Walked. Walked. Now trouble walking. Multi-generational tribal. Quiet. Wife took care of everybody. Children—girl I was fond of. Boy mattered most. Older people. All people I cared about were killed or died from wounds. I had to get away from people who'd seek me out. Nomads and scavengers were looking for weapons and food. Needed to get into a better climate. I had no tent. I had something to start a fire. I picked up the best sword I could find— took off for hundreds of miles. No horse. Took me two years.

"I'm in survival mode. Fire will attract people but repel predators. Can I survive? Get out of this mode? Can I be a soldier for food? I have to do something. I'm used to being a part of traveling along with families; eastern, northern Asian. Didn't think—just survive—be careful. Persevere. I have to be alert—animals of prey and soldiers or survivors who'd want what I have. I picked up a good sword and I know how to use it. Always a struggle. Going to sleep—defenseless. Finding a place between rocks—stoking up a fire."

Awf eventually finds people but they are racially different so he is now the minority. He described them as Asian Mongolian people who have spread across the land from conquest over the last 150 years. "They know I'm no threat," he says. "I won't eat more than I can earn." He said at some point he just wanted to stop being alone as he missed people.

"They know the area and I don't," he said. "We hook up to see how it goes—women, families, soldiers, children, and animals—camp life. They have more than I do. I am a guard assigned to this group. I eat with them. We can communicate some. I wouldn't mind having one of the women but know to take that slow. Women are perfectly capable of stabbing you. We move. We travel. [It was] boring but safe. They seem to accept me to a point. Always looking for grazing land. I'd like a nice horse. I know how to ride and would like to be given a chance to ride and show that.

"We moved every few weeks. [We were to the] north of the Caspian Sea, which is east of the Black Sea, in the southwest of Russia. I'm strong but have abused my body to survive. Nutrition was not good. Hard to relax and trust. Later a battle comes. I'm not one of them. They won't protect me at the expense of their people. I'm aggressive and strong but not supported. It is both infuriating to die like this and a relief to end monotony and loneliness—that rings a bell for me now."

Awf died during a turf battle with other nomadic people. "I wanted to fight," he explained. "I did it all my life." He was cornered and realized no one was going to defend him. He died from multiple stab wounds during close hand-to-hand fighting. "Someone finished me off from the back." His last thoughts were, "It's over. Maybe my spirit will find my family."

In terms of unfinished business, Ann described this as a one-dimensional life. "I didn't have a bigger purpose—adventurer—lost people I cared about—not that caring then is like caring today because of their nomadic lifestyle. Lost continuity. Tried to survive all kinds of danger—snakes, wolves, and natural disasters like turning your ankle. I wasn't a deep thinker—none of us were. I was average. I looked different but I was strong so nobody bothered me. No permanent city. Skin tents. Women did a lot of work. [There was] camaraderie with one's own people. Steal valuables from the dead. Horses were very desirable but unattainable. It would have been exhilarating to ride."

In comparing Awf's life to hers, Ann said they both have wanderlust and a love of horses; a sense of seeking different things. "That part of the world has always attracted me," she said. "There were so many people like that. He was strong. I'm not. I don't get sick. If you were weak then you'd be dead. Eat and ride like now. I could use a bow and arrow."

Ann was struck by the contrast of the loneliness Awf experienced then and the loneliness she feels since losing her husband, Stan. "I'm not lonely now in comparison," she admits. "I'm in a safe place, [can] pick up phone. Good perspective that I'm not one of those people. Makes me think at times that now I'm a big baby, spoiled and self-indulgent. I do stuff. I am not depressed. Back then it was one-dimensional. I was strong. I was ambidextrous. I could use the sword with either [hand]. Not that way now. Totally about survival. Now that Stan is gone, I'm alone and have to figure things out."

In this life, Ann is very interested in archaeology. She enjoys reading about unique items buried by various nomadic Asian peoples, with gravestones that look vaguely humanoid. That gave scientists insights into what those people did, but those gravestones were only for important people. "Reading those articles made me grateful that I had visited those places for myself," she said.

Ann saw this life in a general sense. "It was fairly pointless, not profound," she said. "Maybe having had that, I didn't want to be that. I wanted family. Lost them. Wanderlust was always there. Love of horses. This life educated, a thinking, feeling being in the way we would think about it now. Even as a child, I longed to travel, especially to Asia."

"I realized what people would do who were on the ground fighting people on horseback," she added. "Best thing to do was to cut the left fore leg of the horse to bring down the rider. Barbaric to cut down the animal doing what it is told to do. I have ambulatory issues now. Patch body together. Fleeing loneliness—both lives. Contrast in externals is overwhelming but there are some important themes that have come through. Romanticizes travel – we take so much for granted."

Ann's Soul Writing

It was a waste, pointless. I never knew much love, given or received. I am an eternal being. Quiet. Friendship was dangerous; people did not live long. Why love? Why trust? Eat, drink and be merry. Why did I survive (just like now?) Should have been dead. But don't fight the gods. The fates. They are to be feared. Now I know God is love, goodness. I have grown in development and consciousness. Thank you, God. I'm grateful for that growth for what I have now. I must complete my soul intention in this life before I die; to write, share the love of God with others and not just eat, drink and be merry. Lord, strengthen me. Now I'm a mental person, not just a body. I can do it. I will do it.

My Soul Writing

There are multiple issues contained in this life in terms of physical karma. Some are obvious—having to do with ambulatory challenges. Then that soul had no choice but to walk for hundreds of miles—but it was why he had to walk that matters more than the fact that he incurred problems with legs and feet because of the intensity of the walking. He walked because he was fleeing— he walked to survive. The idea of fleeing being the key here. How does the idea of fleeing play into Ann's life now? What is she running from? It is no longer an army that will destroy her—but something else? The other incident to pay attention to is the idea of always having her/his back to the wall to survive. How has that manifested in this life? Certainly Stan's death put her in the same mindset. Similar to death of Awf's family—idea of back against the wall—need for survival. Death came in that way, too. Could fight what he saw in front of him. What was there, what was obvious—but it was what was behind him that he could not see that caused his demise—i.e. the unknown. He was strong and could fight that which was obvious, but blinded to what wasn't—thus lost his ability to survive—could not survive that which he could not see—some similarities in this life for her to discover and reveal.

When I checked in with Ann about six weeks after our session, she reported no bleed through, but by then she had been diagnosed with breast cancer so her thoughts were focused on what were the roots of her new condition.

In reviewing her body scan, there were several important clues connecting not only Awf's life but also other past lives with her present physical karma. For instance, she flashed back to a Spanish past life in which she saw herself on her hands and knees scrubbing a floor. I asked why she thought that image came to her.

"The Spanish life is very relevant to my present life from knee issues to knowing many of the people in that life now," she said. "Just as my husband died in my present life, he predeceased me in the Spanish life. Plus it's the only female past life I know much about."

Returning to her body scan, I reminded Ann that when she did the scan of her arms, she identified a mole on her middle left finger and said she had encountered two chronic conditions from prior lifetimes, both affecting her upper and lower limbs. She indicated she had been diagnosed with Charcot-Marie-Tooth (neuro-muscular) in college and Dupuytren's Contracture (curls the fingers) in the early 1990s. Both conditions have limited the use of her limbs.

I then asked Ann to review the sensitivities and discomforts she reported in various parts of her body during the scan and to report if any of them tied into Awf's life experience. She said the weakness in her hands and feet; muscle loss in both areas; tension in her neck and shoulders; neck and throat issues; and even eye problems could all relate to Awf's life and to other Central Asian lives she had that were physically hard, dangerous and lonely. "I walked (and rode when I could) thousands of miles, with limited food and water, in a harsh, windy, desert land with sun glare," she explained. "My present weight and reflux issues could even be compensation for my frequent hunger as Awf."

When we were discussing the problems with her hands during the scan, she made the comment, "I'll have to kill fewer people than I did in the past." In addition, she said she did not have any birthmarks, yet she discussed a mole on her middle left finger. I asked if she considered that a birthmark and why did she tie in problems with her hands with her having killed people in the past?

"One usually kills people with hand-held weapons," she said. "It was a frequent case of kill or be killed. I've long wondered about the mole, which is the only mole I have and is on the middle finger, which is used in a gesture of crude sexuality. In Awf's time and much of history, crude and violent sexuality was very common."

A constant theme in Ann's session was having her back up against something—both literally and figuratively. In describing Awf's death she said she was cornered and, "Someone finished me off from the back." I asked how the idea of being backed into a corner, or making sure her back was covered so no one could sneak up on her, had anything to do with her physical karma today. She did not answer the question directly, but instead went back to her understanding of that era. "Times were brutal," she explained. "Rest was often not an option. Nutrition was poor for man and beast. I saw how brutal I could be to my horse in a former regression. Cause and effect."

During the regression, Ann repeatedly talked about the need to have others around her in order to survive—as if she could not survive on her own. I asked how those statements mirrored her current physical karma or issues. She said in this life she is a "roaring extrovert. I like and need people." Reflecting on her life since the unexpected passing of her husband who was her partner in every sense of the word, Ann said she is very lonely living alone, especially with her physical limitations.

One of the other themes in Awf's life was acceptance. I asked Ann if any of those sentiments resonated with her life now and she said her thinking now is so different—even weird—compared to most people, especially her neighbors. "I need to think what and what not to say." It is a common dilemma for metaphysicians everywhere!

During the regression, Ann said that the motivating factor in Awf's travels was the death of his people. At his death, Awf said he was relieved, anticipating he would be reunited with his family. Ann was struck by the loneliness Awf felt and the loneliness she has felt since her husband passed, commenting on the many parallels between Awf's feelings and her feelings about her husband.

"I have a small family," she said. "Most of those I've loved deeply have died. My husband was my helpmate. He could do many things I can't—hence the feelings of not only loneliness but insecurity."

Referring to Awf's life, Ann called it, "fairly pointless, not profound." Yet we both knew from our work in this field that no life is pointless or without some profound meaning. Looking back, I asked Ann if she still believed Awf's life was pointless, or could she now see some meaning in it.

"There's always purpose, but I'm so mental now that there's a huge gap (but still some attraction) between my wild lives and now. Remote Central Asia was some of my favorite travels in this life."

Despite the overwhelming external contrasts between Awf's life and hers, Ann identified several important themes that ran true for both lives, including the geographic fascination with wild Asia, love of horses, dependence versus independence issues, hunger then and overeating now, the pros and cons of freedom—especially being alone and physically limited.

Another insight was the "back to the wall" issue. Awf could fight what he saw in front of him, what was obvious, but it was what was behind him, i.e. the unknown, that he could not see that caused his demise. He was "blinded" to what wasn't obvious—could not survive that which he could not see. I asked Ann if in this life she had a sense of being blinded with her back against the wall.

"I've just been blindsided by the breast cancer," she answered. [Note: I found it interesting that she used the word "blindsided"]. I always thought my husband would outlive me and was glad because he was better equipped to deal with a variety of problems."

Ann said our session impacted her life, but at the time we did the session, it mostly was confirming what she already knew about her Central Asian lives. While her writing reaffirmed her preconceptions, mine, she said, added new depth and was, in her words, "almost precognitive."

I asked what, if any, changes occurred in her physical conditions after our session. Ann said, "My karmic physical issues are deep and chronic; they remain constant. I'm grateful to have participated and to have found some new insights."

Don't be Resentful of Life's Lessons

Christine is a 63-year-old government contractor who came to the project after participating in a group regression I conducted in northern Virginia. She had suffered with foot pain since childhood and had to stop tap dancing because her feet hurt too much. Twenty years ago, she developed lymph edema in the toes of both feet, resulting in having to wear compression stockings. She had heel spur surgery and today wears orthotics. The pads on her feet are "worn out" and she also suffers from arthritis, which plays a part in her foot pain.

Not surprising, during the full-body scan, Christine identified sensitivity in the arch of her right foot and toes and reported a light tingling on top of feet. She felt energy going up and down her left leg, shin, and feet as well as the top of her right knee. She felt sensitivity in the center of her stomach beneath her breast. Her left index finger was throbbing and there was sensitivity in the second finger and below her elbows. She complained of discomfort in her shoulder blades and upper back. Her lower jaw and throat were tight and the front part of her neck felt heavy. The tip of her tongue was burning, but that was always a problem for her. Her head ached but she couldn't tell where the pain was centered.

Christine saw herself in 1915 in Wichita, Kansas as a slender, happy 6-year-old girl with the same first name she has now, but with the last name of O'Brian. She wore black Mary Jane shoes with anklets. Her dress had a flowered pattern with puffed sleeves and a full skirt. Her black hair was long with a slight curl.

Christine lived in a town lined with sidewalks and homes with tiny yards. Her house was small with a long narrow hallway leading to the kitchen. The foyer was adorned with heavy wood, and stairs that went up to the second floor where she slept. To the left of the foyer was a room with a fireplace.

Christine's evening meal consisted of tomato soup sipped from a red bowl. She was seated at a table in the kitchen, swinging her legs. Her mother was there, wearing an apron. She could not pinpoint her feelings about her mother. "I get the impression she's tired," Christine said. "She's wearing a baggy, sack dress. She feels old to me." She did not see or feel the presence of her father or siblings.

When asked about the significant event in that life, Christine saw herself in a beige suit, with a mid-calf length skirt and her short hair tucked under a hat. She was in her 20s. "I'm standing by myself in a bar with three stocky, heavy men in suits—rough looking, intimidating. I'm talking to all of them. It was pre-arranged that I meet them there. I'm standing in the center, feeling surrounded. I light a cigarette so I don't feel so intimidated. I try to feel more in control. I'm the only woman there. I'm trying to set up a bootlegging deal. They are the drivers and I want them to distribute the liquor. It's my liquor—but I don't know its origin. I had a partner [her deceased husband] but he's no longer there. It's the first time I'm trying it out on my own. I'm still scared being the only female in the room with these big, heavyset men, but I seem to be winning them over."

The men agree to her deal and she leaves. "I'm walking down the street. I feel so relieved—trying to survive," she says. "I get tangled up with a little boy who runs into me on a two-wheel bicycle. I'm sitting on the ground. I'm just sobbing—like a release from the tension. Like I lost my husband and this was just the breaking point."

The boy is uninjured and stays with her. An older man from the hardware store comes out and assists her to a bench in front of the store. "I do everything to hide the pain in my legs," Christine says. "Sitting there with him, my pride stops me from admitting that I'm hurt. It is painful, but there is no bleeding so there is nothing you can see that looks hurt. I sat there quite a while. He gave me a handkerchief. I finally got up and walked home. It's not a long walk. I have a very small upstairs apartment. I am sitting on my bed, my legs in front of me, with ice bags on my calves. My roommate comes home and insists I see a doctor. I do but the doctor only pats me on the knee and says I'll be fine. But I'm not fine." This condition persists the rest of her life.

Christine dies from a respiratory problem at an old age. She had been in bed for a long time because her ankles and calves were swollen and she could not walk very well. Her former roommate had a large house and had taken her in. She was with Christine when she passed.

Christine expressed no resentment about that life, but admitted she was disgusted with herself. "I blame my husband for dying; having to take care of myself and being on my own." Her regret was never having children.

When we looked at parallels between the two Christines, the present Christine said, "I escape a lot to my bed. I lay down a lot."

The only person in this life that she identified from the previous life was her former roommate who has been her friend in this life since she was 12. "She's always been my closest friend," she said. "In the previous life she was my caretaker. We're there emotionally for each other."

Christine's Soul Writing

You are not alone. Don't be resentful for life's lessons. They are there to teach you. The fear of being able to take care of yourself is not necessary. You are more than capable and stronger than you can imagine. You have not allowed yourself to see that in this lifetime because of fear. You always have acquired a protector and have done a good job at it but like anything else in life, life changes and you are resisting it from the fear-based thinking of not being good enough to handle situations. Part of the lesson for this marriage, when things get unpleasant you walk away. You escape. Don't escape. Do something about it before you give in. It's hard. You want to hang on but you overlook many things.

My Soul Writing

The significance of leg injuries for Chris is that it has "crippled" her in more ways than physical. It has stopped her from moving forward physically, emotionally, and spiritually and put her instead in a position of blame. She was already embittered by the time she faced the group of men. She had to do that because it was the only way she could survive. She "stood" in the midst of them, hoping her legs would get her out of there if need be, or enable her to stand strong and endure the meeting. They did both—serving her well. She was so relieved and feeling liberated that she was careless in where she walked. She described the accident as being entangled in that bike. She got twisted to the point of incurring internal injuries, which went undetected by the doctor's cursory examination. Being untreated, the condition grew worse until she was unable to get around much. So it is in this life that the remnants of the injury serve as a reminder to stand on our own two feet, to not be reliant on others, to move out of a situation when it does not feel right, to always be aware of one's surroundings, to not blame others for her immobility. This condition actually started in a prior lifetime. It is her legs and feet that symbolize whatever issues or stage in life she finds herself. They are all connected. Finding that common thread will help her to see the bigger picture and when this is done she can learn the lesson intended. Understand the connection between the physical and the emotional and the spiritual. Once learned the pattern will discontinue.

Christine described foot pain in both her initial questionnaire and in the body scan. In her past life, she described the accident that produced life-long issues with her legs. She also said her pride prevented her from admitting she was hurt. That same attitude has emerged again in this life, manifesting as a fear of standing on her "own two feet."

During the regression, she talked about meeting those intimidating men when she was trying to set up a deal to buy her liquor. She was frightened, but interestingly enough, managed to stand on her own two feet. I asked if that memory had anything to do with her current chronic condition.

"As a child I was extremely afraid of conflict of any kind," she answered. "My worst fear as a young adult was to confront someone if they overcharged me or if they made a mistake. I could not express myself. Having three children and marrying the person I did changed that. I learned how to fight and stand up for myself."

Revisiting her body scan, I sensed that the tightness in her lower jaw around her neck and throat, the burning tongue and heaviness in her neck tied in with her past-life experience and she agreed, saying it represented her being able to express herself and handle stress.

Christine indicated that in this life she fell in a warehouse and needed knee replacements, but said she was "always in fear." I asked if those sentiments resonated to her in this life and if so, how were they manifesting in terms of the physical conditions she was experiencing.

"After having this session, it has become a wake-up call for me," she answered. "By eating better foods, it has allowed me to walk more. I was fearful of even walking! I have purchased a Fitbit and become more aware of just what I can do and not what I can't do. It's become a matter of taking back my power and not looking at myself as a victim."

In Christine's soul writing, she was encouraged to not walk away from unpleasant situations. I asked if she saw the connection with the statements, "don't walk away" or "don't escape" with her foot/knee/leg problems.

"I have had to ask myself the question as to why I have made certain choices in my life and for what reasons, good and bad," she admitted. "I have taken these statements to heart and recognized those times when I do need time alone and those times that I have given up and escaped. By seeing the difference, it has changed my energy level. It has changed my concept of myself (raising my consciousness). I have set boundaries and no longer am living in fear."

The significance of her leg injuries was the fact that it crippled her in more ways than one. It stopped her from moving forward physically, emotionally, and spiritually and instead put her in a position of blame. She acknowledged that was a true statement. "I have blamed everyone and myself," she said. "I have been resentful of things that I have allowed to happen. This session has changed that for me."

I also found it probable that in this life the remnants of the injury were serving as a reminder to not be reliant on others, to move out of a situation when it doesn't feel right, to always be aware of her surroundings and not blame others for her immobility.

"I have learned from this that if a situation does not feel right, instead of escaping, it is up to me to change it," she said. "Express my complaint and teach those around me the difference between complaining and criticism. One is constructive. One is destructive. Take the lead in making a change. This way if change doesn't occur, then they are left behind, so to speak."

In terms of how she processed information during the regression, Christine said her emotions arose at the time of the session, but in going back and reviewing it, they were just as strong. "I was amazed how I remembered feeling that there was no filter in what I was saying. Understanding happened in stages," she reflected. "The clarity in the images is just as strong today as when I had the regression."

Christine said she had no prior knowledge of this life-time and that the soul-writing portion of the session gave her a sense of knowing. "It was coming from a place I have not experienced except through past-life regression," she said. Her soul writing also helped to explain her strong desire to have children in this life. "I felt it is what I always wanted to do," she said. "I feel the same about my grandchildren. I want to have a big impact on their lives."

Overall, Christine said the session gave her compassion towards one daughter that has fought a battle with ADD with very little understanding and support from her. "She knows now that she has an advocate and can help her more." Christine also said the session enabled her to learn to put more joy in her life rather than it being a battle with fear.

In looking at her chronic condition before and after the regression, Christine said it did not go away completely, but it had improved substantially. "This has been a life changer for me," she said. "It has made me honestly look at myself and take responsibility for my life. I have a responsibility to myself to move only forward. It is a journey that only I can do. It has brought me closer to my daughters. I have always had a good relationship with them, but it is stronger now. Life is now on my terms. Compromises are made but not a level of self-sacrifice."

[Note: Christine identified this time period as 1915 and said she died of old age at 80, meaning she would have died in 1995. Clearly that life would have overlapped her current life, making her recollection of the time period problematic. In terms of what she gained from this session, having the time period accurate is not the issue but rather the symbolism of the leg injury is more important to focus on.]

Chapter Three

It's All in Your Head

"Mind becomes the builder. The physical body is the result."
(Edgar Cayce Reading 3359-1)

Migraines, allergies, vision issues, throat and neck problems—just a few of the many maladies associated with physical karma involving the head. This was an area of study I was especially interested in, as I had been dealing with throat karma for some time in the early days of my work. While I never had a problem expressing myself in writing, I was unable to spontaneously verbalize what I knew so well when standing at a podium in front of an audience. I had to have any number of prompts with me, including a detailed script, which I boringly read to the audience. The pattern was clear. Every time I stood up to "speak my truth" my throat would close up and I could barely get a word out. Why was that, I wondered?

I later learned that I had multiple throat traumas in previous lives, each time having something to do with my spiritual work. It was no wonder that when I attempted to share my knowledge that nothing came out of my mouth. It was as if my karmic memory was reminding me—"Oh no! Remember what happened the last time you did this!"

I've managed to work my way through that to a certain extent, although occasionally I do draw a blank. It is then that I am reminded of the origin of that fear—a fear that is common among healers and those who step out of the box to continue the work they began centuries earlier.

The Bible is filled with references to karmic retribution, i.e., "an eye for eye, and tooth for tooth." Cayce found that in his work as well, telling a 33-year-old blind musician that his blindness stemmed from actions in a Persian lifetime when he used hot irons to blind members of other tribes.

This chapter presents the past-life journeys of three women suffering from head-related issues, including Naomi, whose death from being pushed down a stone stairway in an ancient lifetime has resulted in a pattern of repeatedly being hit from behind in this life; Teresa, who is hearing impaired in this life, going to a 19th century life in Kentucky where she ignored advice and direction from her parents; and Cecilia, whose loss of voice in this life originates from a 19th century Native American life in which her cries for help were ignored.

Why Remain Apart?

Naomi is a 64-year-old retired associate vice president and university administrator. She complained of chronic arthritis in her neck and spine, but added that a few months earlier she blacked out when she had the flu and suffered a concussion. She came to the project because she saw repeating patterns in her life.

Naomi's regression took her to what she believed to be 5 B.C. in either Egypt or Greece. She saw herself as Orelia, a tall, slender female in her 20s with olive skin. She wore gold sandals with thin straps. Her three-quarter-length white dress had multiple folds and a gold sash and it flowed gently as she walked. She had long, straight, smooth black hair and wore a small gold crown encrusted with jewels.

Orelia lived in a place that was hilly and sparse, with trees and gardens. She described the climate as Mediterranean—not too hot or cold—but cooler in the buildings. From her vantage point high on a hillside, she overlooked a white stonewall that led down to a large courtyard.

"Where I am is part of a big building—a lot of people live there," she said. "It feels like a palace. Floors and walls are stone. Windows are cut out. No coverings. Walls are thick, cool and relatively smooth. Water is below in ponds. I'm part of a community." She felt she was in a privileged position, but did not want to claim it.

Orelia ate from a hammered-out wooden plate with a large edge around it. She used utensils and drank out of a goblet. Her father, a gray-haired man dressed in fancy clothing, was eating with her, as were other members of her community.

"We're in a long narrow room with windows all around," she explained. "I'm at the head of the table and the rest are seated around the table, but I am apart from them. They are talking to each other. I have no connection to them. It's almost as if I'm watching, being apart emotionally, disconnected. It's as if I am somehow set aside in importance."

At this point in the session, Naomi kept hearing the phrases, "Apart from" and "Not rejected." She acknowledged she was seen as more important than the others, but again insisted she did not know why.

Orelia's significant event was the result of the jealousy others felt toward her. She was still young, in her late 20s, and clearly remembered being deliberately pushed down a curved stone stairway. She did not see who came up behind her, but said she felt her body slamming against the hard stone, resulting in a fatal head injury.

"It's a long staircase," she explained. "I'm lying on the stairs blacked out. I'm taken to a bed. I see the old man and I'm lying there. I think I lingered for a while. I see people running around but I think I might be dead because I'm up above watching this."

Her last thoughts were, "I was glad to escape because I was always set apart from everybody and lonely. I wondered who pushed me."

The theme of that life was Orelia's inability to control her destiny. She had been identified as someone vastly different from her peers and that resulted in jealousy and envy. She felt this was undeserved as she was never cruel or mean to anyone.

Karmically this has played out in Naomi's life in several ways, including the pattern of repeatedly being hit from behind, feeling separated from others and not knowing how to be her authentic self without incurring unwarranted jealousy. As an example, she said a male co-worker pushed her from behind to get her out of the way when they were racing out of a building during the Mineral, VA earthquake. She also had multiple car accidents in which she was hit from behind.

"I've always felt like an observer and apart from my (birth) family; making up for that by being smarter and more capable; by being in charge and caring for them, but it didn't get me any closer to them," she said. "People have a strong reaction to me. If I'm playing my role of being capable, there is jealousy and backstabbing. Power plays happened to me several times at work. People who loved me really loved me, but there were small circles of other people who reacted to a powerful personality or other parts of me that brought out jealousy in them. In this life I am trying to find a way of connection."

Naomi's Soul Writing

Soul unity. Stream of thought. Why remain apart? Be myself. Be with yourself and accept the power. Do not hide it, squash it, be lost or regret. Be who you are, God has made you for a purpose, for meaning for helping others. You must give up feeling apart— better to take your role and quit judging yourself and everyone else. Accept your place. Accept inside and out everything. Every natural possession. Every intelligence. Every thought, every quirk, every bit of yourself and then you will be in a place where you don't judge others and will be in the flow of your true purpose. Quit trying to figure it all out. Just be. Just be. Just be who you are in this and other lives. You are a victim only because you do not accept yourself—sets you up for jealousy, hate, conflict, resistance. Give up resistance and light floods in. You are magnificent, powerful, holy and good and that is your purpose/path and you must align with it. Resistance only harms you and others.

My Soul Writing

Because of her preferred status—one thrust upon her rather than one she earned—she enraged those who were subservient to her who felt she had usurped their rightful place. The only way for them to take her place was if she died. They conspired against her and designated whoever was around her first to do the deed.

These souls are still in her life today—the same souls in this life who have shown jealousy toward her. The head and neck injury today are reminders of the treachery of the past, to warn her to see these souls for who they are and to avoid putting herself in harm's way. Knowing this pattern continues, she can transcend it through forgiveness work and by identifying those souls—then and before—who wish her pain and keeping herself apart from them on a physical level, but forgiving them on a spiritual level to transmute the karma so the pattern ceases.

Naomi reported having received additional insights after the session. These came in the form of conscious imagining and connection of current life situations to the previous life where she noted patterns of feeling apart and then being attacked from behind. I asked if the comments Orelia made at dinner—feeling, "apart from" but "not rejected" by her community, had any meaning for her in this life.

"Yes," she said, "especially in the context of my recent career/work environment where I was 'apart from' those I supervised and those who supervised me. A feeling of separateness. I always have felt different from the majority of people, including my immediate family, yet able to blend in through superficial appearances or through actions trying to participate or be like others. In my efforts to be nice or liked, I did not exert my power fully, but tried to compromise or exert power in less direct communicative ways."

The significant event in Orelia's life was her death. This brought up the recurrent issue of having people doing something to her behind her back; and as a result, being hit and having a head injury. I asked Naomi to look at Orelia's life and her own and expand on the similarities between the two.

"I have had repeated occurrences over my working life of me 'being me' and assuming the good in others and that things are fine, or at least 'assuming' neutral or good feelings in relationships—only later to be turned on, behind my back, and attacked," she said. "Each time I was surprised at the meanness and often who it was. It was upsetting and shocking; very disheartening. The whiplash injuries to my neck occurred while at red lights. The most recent was someone running a red light and totaling my car on the right side. When I hit my head I passed out, resulting in both a significant concussion and another neck injury. So—[the pattern is] minding my own business and getting these surprise attacks as I innocently go about my business."

Jealousy and envy were recurrent themes in this session. Orelia felt as though her life was out of her control and I wondered if Naomi felt the same about her life and she did.

"As I said, being nice or kind, but in positions of authority, ended up in envy/jealousy and attacks," she explained. "How others feel about me seems largely out of my control as I can't control perceptions/feelings/reactions to me. How I see myself may be very different from how some others see me."

In her soul writing Naomi questioned why she should remain apart. Her higher self encouraged her to be herself, accept her power and not hide it. Since our session, I asked if she thought about that advice and ways to embrace it.

"I am in transition—retired recently, recovering from a concussion, moved, lost my mother, etc.," she explained. "So I bowed out of the position of authority and expertise I had for the last 14+ years. I certainly have thought of embracing myself and personal power in this new life—embracing my artistic capabilities as well as Healing Touch practitioner skills. I'm reinventing myself without the traditional career structure, so hopefully I can accept this new power of simply being myself and claiming any skills, abilities, etc."

Naomi's writing indicated that she was the one setting herself apart. In my writing it appeared that role was thrust upon her. Looking back, I asked which she thought it was (or is it a little of both) and what did that mean in terms of her life today.

"My innate abilities, skills, and personality placed me in that role," she said. "I set myself apart by not embracing the position or allowing myself to be in authority. This is the same as in this life—able and capable, but holding back so others will like me. It didn't always work!"

It appeared that many of the souls from Orelia's life are in Naomi's life now, repeating the same pattern as before. When patterns from one life are so strongly repeated in a subsequent life, there is a great lesson there. I asked Naomi if she saw the pattern and what had she learned from it.

"Yes—I see the pattern," she said. "My tendency is to avoid being in the limelight and instead to seek like-minded people and those with similar strengths. Perhaps this would avoid being singled out, attacked and misunderstood. Maybe, maybe not! I suppose I could be 'out there' with more people, rather than trying to blend in while actually squashing myself."

Naomi reported that after our session her condition remained about the same, but that it was improving with her use of several healing modalities. "I am grateful for the experience," she said.

Learning to Pay Attention

In this life, 53-year-old Teresa was born hearing impaired in both ears and although it was an inherited condition, she was not diagnosed nor fitted with hearing aids until she was eight.

Her body scan picked up a cold feeling in her feet, with some throbbing on her right foot under the second and third toes on the pad of her foot. She likened the feeling to stepping on a stone. She said it felt as though her right leg wasn't there and it didn't seem as solid as her left. She had an ache on the right side of her back and felt nauseated the moment I asked her to scan her kidneys and bladder. When we scanned her chest, she reported a shortness of breath and a slight heaviness in the heart area. There was tingling in the base of her thumb and palm of her right hand and her right arm felt numb from the elbow down. When asked to scan her spine, her whole body became sensitized and she shivered. In her neck she felt the kind of pressure one would get if wearing a brace from ear-to-ear. Finally, she reported a concentration of pain in her third eye area between her brows.

Teresa regressed to the year 1858 in Kentucky where she saw herself as a tall, scrawny, 18-year-old by the name of Sam Jenkins. Sam was tan, with strong, work-worn hands that had broken nails and calluses. His feet were bare and he was wearing pants held up with a rope. He had on a loose shirt and no underclothes. His short, thick, coarse hair was light brown and covered by a straw hat.

Sam was in the woods but could see a clearing ahead. A farmstead with a fenced area, small barn, a well, and a one-story log house with a chimney and loft were off in the distance.

Sam ate his evening meal sitting at a table on a rough, plank stool. He was eating gruel that had been sitting over the fire all day. "I'm hungry. It's all I have," he says. He ate out of a wooden bowl with a utensil that had a handle and was flat and rounded as a spoon, but resembled a scraper.

When asked if anyone was eating with him, he began to cry and started talking in a heavy southern dialect. "They're gone—dead," he sobbed. "My parents and sister. I try not to think about it because I can't do anything about it. Just keep farmstead going. Animals all died. They all got sick and died. I wasn't there. [I was] out in the woods. I wasn't doing what I was supposed to do—hunting, looking for food. Gone for a few days. They got sick and by the time I got back, my ma and sister were in bed dying. Dad was trying to care for them. He tried to care for the animals, the cow. He told me to try to make something out of the cow to help my sister and mother. He died, too. Wolves came and got that cow."

Sam became very despondent after this, suffering from enormous guilt. He went through the motion of going out finding wild eggs and hunting small game. He gathered wheat and grains that were planted. He didn't farm—just let them grow wild and harvested what was there. He was slowly starving to death. He did not have the means to go to another homestead or town. Even if he did, he had too much pride to ask for help. By then the cabin was in such disarray that to the outside world it looked abandoned. No one came to check on him and he lived in isolation.

Most of the time Sam wandered the woods, looking for food to appease his constant hunger. When he wasn't wandering, he'd sit in the cabin and replay in his mind the death of his family and what he could have done to change it. He kept asking himself why he wasn't there and as a result suffered from much self-recrimination. He tried to be self-sufficient, but he didn't know how to do anything, including making candles or mending his clothes. He felt as though he was not good enough to have a wife or any type of female companionship, adding that nobody was interested in him because he didn't have anything, although he added that he may have "cleaned up good" had he cared enough to try.

When he ran out of bullets and wasn't able to hunt anymore, he walked into the woods and died from exposure at the age of 20. His last thoughts were remorse. "Sorry, Ma. Sorry, Pa. I couldn't do it anymore," he cried.

He later explained that when his family became ill he had been in the woods, escaping his duties, chores and responsibilities.

"Dad was to take care of the homestead and I was to go out and hunt," he said. "I didn't like the effort or discipline it took to hunt. Dad had the rifle. I had to use the knife and bow. I wasn't very good at the bow. I could throw a knife better."

Teresa could relate to Sam's lack of discipline and refusal to accept responsibility and commitment; i.e., "Knowing there has to be something done and procrastinating and not doing it," she said.

What Sam didn't realize was that his family died of food poisoning, an insight that Teresa got later. "I'm getting a picture of molded grain or a mistaken mushroom/herb for flavoring." Nonetheless, Sam rationalized that it was his fault because he did not heed his father's instructions. It was clear Teresa's karmic hearing issue in this life stemmed from Sam's inability to hear his father's orders about his responsibility to his family.

In terms of individuals from Sam's life who are in her life now, Teresa felt her daughter in this life was Sam's mother, her younger son was Sam's sister, and her ex-husband was Sam's father.

Her daughter was not playing a role in her life now and the issue of abandonment was playing itself out between the two of them. Teresa understands this, recalling that Sam's mother often left him alone as a child to help her husband. Once Sam was mobile, his mother would leave him to do household chores. There was minimum necessary contact between them other than feeding. He saw her death as the ultimate abandonment. Teresa's relationship with her daughter in this life is repeating this pattern, as there isn't much contact between the two of them.

Teresa's Soul Writing

Life hard. Escape to the forest, woods. Escape. Dreamer. Don't want to work on homestead. Don't know anything else but there is something else out there. Where in woods is it? Ma, Pa love each other. Worked hard together to build homestead. Don't understand why I don't have same drive, desire to do as well. Sister, love her, watched her more than ma did especially when ma lost other baby and was sick afterwards. Heard her crying and pa was carrying on how it was his fault for making her work so hard. Was easier before they came out to start again. Pa felt like a failure cuz he couldn't keep ma and me fed and in clothes. We had only those things he/they got from the wedding back east to use. Ma used her wedding dress for Katie's dresses and nappies. Too poor to go to town and buy stuff. Had to do with what we had. Not hearing ma/pa call. They called me to come and do chores or eat and I am ignoring them—learning to ignore sounds of lovemaking— ignore sounds of when bear and bobcats around homestead got chickens early on. Got goat too. Cow could defend itself and was kept penned in barn most times. Ma didn't know how to treat sickness. Katie (sister) got it first and then ma, then pa. Katie died first. Dirt floor, loft where I slept was where ma/pa slept when alive. I started sleeping there. Care of animals/wolves at door scared of being on floor myself. Winters hard. Used up stored food ma made and hid from animals. Had to restrain/stop myself from using during spring/summer/fall when could gather. Ran out finally. Too weak to gather more.

My Soul Writing

Sam was a dreamer. While he was loved by his parents and sister, he spent most of his time in his head, envisioning what his life would be like away from the homestead. He focused on that morning, noon and night, which was a source of frustration and irritation to his father who had come to rely on him more and more. Sam did not follow instructions well. He did not pay attention to learn how to be self-sufficient despite numerous attempts to teach him. He went thru life thinking he'd always be taken care of, so why bother to learn anything. That's why when everyone died he had no means of self-preservation. While he could have sought help—which would have been given to him—his pride prevented him from reaching out to anyone and his guilt compelled him to feel as though everything was his fault and he deserved no help. Life was doling out to him what he deserved. At this point even if he wanted to learn how to care for himself and his property, it would not have worked because his lack of discipline and ability to apply himself to hard work would have prevented him from doing so. In recognizing these traits and the price they cost Sam, Teresa can transmute this karma, heal that life and hers, and move forward with a new outlook on life (attitude) and escape

*the guilt and sense of despondency and giving up that destroyed
Sam's young life.*

Nearly two months after our session, Teresa reported having experienced some bleed through having to do with a scent in the air that she smelled shortly after coming out of the regression.

"I have since been 'told' that it is/was rose water," she explained. "I never smelled rose water before and have the feeling that Sam's mother used it often—at least in the beginning," she surmised. "She was disappointed that there were no rose bushes where they lived so that she could have made more. It was a comforting scent that reminded her of their life before moving west."

When Teresa described the parallels between her life and Sam's, she referenced a lack of discipline; accepting responsibility; commitment; as well as being prone to procrastination. I asked how those qualities were manifesting in her current life.

"Most obvious is the weight that I had gained from early in my marriage," she said. "Even after gastric by-pass surgery, I have not been able to get below a threshold and reach my preferred weight. The discipline and commitment to myself to exercise and eat healthy regularly always has been a struggle for me; short term, but never a long-term permanent commitment."

Another theme she identified was not accepting the responsibility of being a mother and caretaker to her children, including the housework and nurturing they required for healthy lives.

A third issue was completing what she starts. "Procrastination and lack of discipline permeates my whole life on many levels and not just the physical," she said. "It shows up in my employment, my spiritual practices, my creative endeavors, and my relationships."

Teresa brought up issues of Sam's mother abandoning him by often leaving him alone as a child and then ultimately dying and that her daughter now was repeating that pattern. While that is not symptomatic of anything she listed as a chronic condition, it is an interesting pattern and I encouraged her to share her thoughts about this and how, in her mind, it connected.

"Simple," she replied. "My mother was overwhelmed with the care of three babies in three years. As the first born, the attention was given to the younger siblings as they came, since I was older and they needed more than I did. At times I also would be responsible for my younger siblings, as it would be too much for my mother, for whatever reason. There eventually would be six of us, with the youngest being born when I was 11. Although I did not have the same birth dynamics when my children were born, I too found myself weaning my older daughter with less attention and eventually also my sons when I had to return to the workforce. My daughter also was thrust into being responsible for her younger brothers until I got home from work. This is repeated as adults. I find that I have abandoned my parents even though they are still living and a few hours away, just as my daughter and older son have 'abandoned' me for probably the same reasons. Namely, 'you do not need us in your life anymore, so therefore we do not need you in ours. We each have more important or higher priority things to take care of.'"

The realization that Teresa's younger son might be the same soul as Sam's sister caused Teresa to become very emotional and she cried at the thought she would lose him. I asked her to elaborate on what emotion that brought up and why she had that concern in this life.

"There was such a strong feeling of grief and loss," she explained. "That as the older, responsible person it was my responsibility to ensure that nothing bad happens. With the marriage separation, my son now lives the majority of his time with his father. Yet there is the feeling that I could not help him, could not be there with or for him. Am not involved in his life—he has left me. As Sam, Katie's death, somehow, is his fault for not being there."

Reviewing her body scan, I asked Teresa to look at each sensitivity, discomfort or birthmark and ascertain if there was any tie in with Sam's life experience that would explain why she continues to deal with them in this life.

"What comes to mind is what the body may do when it has been poisoned or starved," she said. "Being the right side seemed to be more affected with a sense of invisibility, I seem to think it has to do with the fact Sam was lying on his left side curled up when dying. Only the left side was in contact with something solid—the earth—and still felt sensations."

In listening to her recount her life as Sam, it was clear he liked to daydream and could not pay attention and follow instructions. I asked Teresa if that related at all to who she is today or more so, to the chronic conditions she is facing.

"With the hearing loss, I had to learn to pay attention, not only to body language, but also to learn to lip read, and trust that sixth-intuitive sense," she said. "This was a survival skill. However, when the instructions were not followed or under-stood, it led to an easy out. I can't hear so it was assumed that the mistake was made because of it. It also enables the poor deaf girl who can't be self-sufficient and must depend on others. I can safely ignore other people and situations. Sam had good hearing but did not want to listen. Now, I want to listen, but do not have the hearing. Self-sufficiency didn't happen until I was 50 years old and separated from my husband. Until that I time, I depended on everyone else to take care of me."

Sam admitted being prideful and that is what prevented him from reaching out to anyone; that his guilt compelled him to feel as though everything was his fault and he deserved no help. I asked Teresa how that tied into her present condition.

"Being hearing impaired meant that I belonged to neither the deaf community nor the hearing community," she explained. "I was defective in both, could not be identified as part of either community and because of it, would not ask for help. Prideful? Perhaps. It was only through my own efforts that I would make it through this world. If something did not go the way I wanted it to go, it would be my fault and it would be up to me, only me, to fix it. There also was the reflection that my hearing loss was a smirch on my parents' social standing; that somehow I had to pretend that it didn't exist and be as normal and perfect as I possibly could be so as not to ruin their life."

The overall lesson of this lifetime appears to be that it is never too late to make conscious changes in the directions of one's life. I asked Teresa whether she saw that as a possibility in this life.

"Yes, it is not only a possibility, but I am taking the steps to heal this," she answered. "Through therapy, both traditional talk and integrative/holistic, I have been able to change the mindset that supported the despondency and fatalistic view that had this life on course for the same destruction as Sam's. Being involved in shamanic practice also helps with honoring my commitments, following through and being responsible for my actions and their results. I am also making the effort to reconnect with my family."

This was Teresa's first introduction to Sam and she said knowing about this past-life aspect had a significant impact on her life. "The verification that this baggage was not something that I picked up in this lifetime, but have carried from a previous life helped, in a strange way, for me to heal it," she said. "Knowing where it came from allowed me to work with it and, along with shamanic healing sessions, help to understand, accept and let go the energies. To me, my life energies seem lighter and less dark and heavy than before the session. This translates to more open, less hostile interactions and acceptance of my hearing loss as something that is needed to be experienced for my soul's growth and understanding. Not a punishment for something that I did wrong or failed to do. The issue of abandonment had to be faced and healed with the knowledge that I am never alone. Something that had never occurred to me before. Along with this knowledge is that I am perfect in the way that I am—however that physically manifests."

Teresa reported that the physical condition(s) she reported prior to the regression and soul-writing session had remained the same, but she had gained a new perspective.

"I have always been bitter and angry about my hearing loss—never being good or bad enough to be a part of either the deaf or hearing worlds," she said. "Part of this is perhaps caused by Sam's choice to live in his head and selectively hear what is going on around him and has now manifested in this lifetime as a hearing loss. The fear of abandonment and being self-sufficient is something else that has manifested and is in the process of healing. A strength of purpose and confidence that yes, I CAN do this has grown within. That it's okay to ask and receive help and it does not mean that you are defective or diminished in asking for it. Commitment, discipline and responsibility are more difficult to assess, and seem to be ongoing and as yet not totally resolved."

Swallowed By Fear

Speech impairment is often rooted in a previous life in which the individual suffered trauma that impacted his or her ability to talk. Having one's tongue cut out, throat slashed or being hanged has been traced to numerous cases of voice maladies.

Cecilia is a 68-year-old retired nurse/energy practitioner. Several years prior to our meeting, she began to lose her voice—not completely, but where it would suddenly become very faint and hard for others to hear. She described it as "hoarseness" but added she was not sure that was an accurate description. "It's like my throat would be physically blocked from being able to speak in a louder clearer tone," she said. She could not link it to anything specific, but said it was very noticeable and she never knew when it would return. While she was unsure whether this was past-life related, she wanted to find out. "Previous experiences with this kind of work have been helpful to me and I would like to explore the cause of losing my voice to see if it would give me any insights that would be useful."

Cecilia's body scan revealed a considerable amount of discomfort and sensitivity in nearly all parts of her body, starting at her feet where she described an ache at the base of her left big toe, and tightness in her right ankle up into her legs. She described a slight sensation on the right side of her right knee, and on her right thigh, four inches above her kneecap. This was the location of an injury she incurred in this life when she fell out of a tree. The sensation subsided after the scan, but returned when she scanned her right hip. She momentarily felt a strong indigestion discomfort around her solar plexus but dismissed it as something that comes and goes.

Once into her spine, she made an unusual statement, saying she was not feeling her spine physically but was getting images of a small, square, dark block in her neck. She acknowledged a sensation in her right shoulder, but that sensation shifted to tightness in the muscle where her neck and arm joined the shoulder.

She felt something gripping the back of her neck; a small area tightening on the right side of her neck below her jaw line. The square on her neck had changed its shape, but it still felt dark to her. "I felt tearful when I thought about my neck," she said. "I can feel tightness in the back of my neck, too, like someone is putting pressure on the left side. It's uncomfortable. I want them to take their thumb off it."

As she finished her scan, she reported a small irregular red stain on her right eyelid down to her eyebrow. She described it as vertical in shape, longer than wide, irregularly shaped and bright red.

Cecilia's soul took her to the year 1817 in which she was Hardatha, a 17-year-old Native American woman in the Shenandoah Valley of Virginia. Hardatha was tall and strong with long, slender hands that she described as "pretty, haven't done hard work." She had light brown skin and wore her soft, black hair in braids. Her feet were covered with torn leather shoes from which her left foot protruded. Her long, white dress was made from an animal skin, with bright colored beads on the bodice.

Hardatha lived in a "beautiful valley with mountains in the distance; very colorful." She did not see any buildings initially. "I'm sitting on a rock and resting from a very long walk. I sense I'm trying to get away from something. Seems like a mismatch—my white outfit so pristine but the covering on my left foot looks really worn, like I've been walking a long time."

In discussing her evening meal, Hardatha said she was alone and cooking a rabbit over a fire. "I was really hungry—eating it all as soon as it was cooked. I think I haven't eaten in a while. I'm looking over my shoulder. I'm afraid somebody is going to come. I want to put out the fire so they don't find me."

Cecilia saw the significant event right away. The first image was of Hardatha's horse being tied by the ankle. "They're going to hurt my beautiful horse," she said. I asked who "they" were and she replied, "Jealous women in the tribe. They don't like that I am treated better. They want to punish me. I'm the daughter of the chief so I don't have to work like they do. It's not my fault I'm the daughter of the chief—that's just the way it is. They resent me."

When asked what was her father's reaction to the way these women felt, she didn't think he knew. "I'm his favorite. I don't do anything wrong in his eyes. I can make their life harder if I want. I crossed the line. I did make their life harder and they hate me. I stole their sweethearts because I'm very beautiful. Warriors wouldn't pay attention to them if I was around and showed any interest."

And show an interest she did, seducing five warriors. "I liked the attention," she admitted. "I didn't know at first the impact on the other women but even when I did know it didn't stop me. Then it got out of hand. It was like a game. I convinced the warriors to do risky things; dangerous games to prove their manhood and they died. I see them with something leather like a sling with a rock to swing and release against each other. That killed one of them. Then a race to a cliff where they pulled up real short. One couldn't stop and went over the cliff. Another challenge had them crossing a river where it was too swift and two of them drowned. Then there was only one left. He was willing to prove he was the strongest and best, no matter what I asked of him. I see him hanging by a rope. I wanted him to test the strength of his neck with the rope. His neck wasn't as strong. I could do whatever I wanted. That's just how life and death situations were."

When asked about the impact of losing five warriors from the tribe, Hardatha said: "My father has plenty of other warriors and he's busy, so he lets me be, but the women have had enough. They want to kill me. I run and I take my horse. I'm a very good rider. I was riding the horse and they set a trap to catch me. They caught the horse around the ankle and it stopped him short. I fell off. It was so tight around the ankle. I couldn't get it free. I landed in bushes. I got scratched but I wasn't really hurt. My foot got caught and tore the shoe leather. My horse is hurt. I don't have any way to free him and they're coming. I can't help the horse. I start running. I left my beautiful horse in pain."

The scene she described where she is eating rabbit around the campfire occurred several days after this event.

"Somehow I knew I couldn't go back because even my father couldn't protect me," she said. "The women had nothing to lose and they wanted me dead."

Cecilia said at this point her heart hurt, manifesting as a slight pressure in her chest. "I feel that as I am looking at her. She's all about her own survival. She doesn't care about anything else. She's used to being waited on so she doesn't have so many skills. She had to try to do what she observed of the tribal people who did the work—make weapons to hunt for food—she watched but never did it. That beautiful valley doesn't seem so pretty when alone and hunted, wandering around, no place to be, scary."

Then Hardatha spoke again, saying: "I'm always looking over my shoulder but I don't see anybody. I just feel that pressure around my heart—high level of adrenalin, fearful place. No one to help me. Can't go back. Out in wilderness. Where do I go? I'm hungry, afraid and tired. It's dark except for the moon. I know there are animals out there and I can be their prey."

Hardatha wished she could just die. She eventually was found a month later by a warrior from another tribe. She experienced what it was like to be powerless and enslaved and at the mercy of somebody else's games. "I was pretty much near death because I couldn't take care of myself. He threw me over his horse and brought me back as if to say, "look what I found." I couldn't understand anything they said. They knew I was of no use to them in the condition I was in. They fed me and took care to get my strength back so I could be of use to them and make me work hard. I didn't want to live like this. Many weeks later I tried to run away. They caught me. I see marks on my back. They tied me up and beat me with a branch or a hide. I'm begging to be free, begging for kindness that I did not give to others. I feel remorse for how I treated others."

She remained in captivity for months. "I think they grew tired of me because I wasn't of much use and they wanted to move on," she said. "I see myself tied to a post or tree and just left there and they move on. I'm helpless. I can't get away. I'm all alone. I scream for help but no help comes."

She is 18-years-old at the time. Tied to that post, she dies of a combination of starvation and cold.

Her last thoughts were, "I'm so sorry. I would have been kinder. I didn't know how cruel and hurtful I had been. My left thigh is really aching. My legs are tired, achy and hurt. I'm tied pretty tightly to that post. Sensitivity in my chest is just the terror of being alone. I'm totally vulnerable. I cried out for help for so long, I lost my voice and despaired no help was coming."

In examining the parallels to her present life, Cecilia said, "It's almost the opposite—like trying to make up—always trying to take care of people sometimes at the expense of myself. In recent years I experienced a dread being out in the woods— even though in this life I spent a lot of time in the woods as a kid and I wasn't afraid."

Cecilia felt emotion throughout the session. Knowing how she was then made her sick to her stomach. She equated her ankle being held as the struggle for freedom in this life. Her voice was strong one minute and then gone the next. She said fear swallows her voice. When she faces fear, her voice comes back quickly.

Cecilia's Soul Writing

Revulsion. How selfish and cruel I was grips me in the solar plexus. Feel sick "to my stomach." Grief held in my ankle. Some things are worth the risk standing up for.

Isolation is deadly and the most thing to fear.

Breathe. The neck and shoulder do not need to carry such great fear anymore.

Use my legs more. They can carry me far if I take care of them.

Animals more loyal than I was.

Voice swallowed by fear.

As fears lessen voice becomes stronger.

Pay attention to my body messages, it will guide me if I'm walking in trust.

Stop running. Now is the time to live free of the past.

That's all for now.

....

Cecilia was able to attribute current discomfort and sensitivity in her body with injuries sustained by her past-life aspect. When we did the body scan, she complained of a tingling discomfort in her knees and left hip, both of which she later said was the result of Hardatha's fall from her horse. Her difficulty in breathing, she said, was due to the crying and fear she felt knowing the tribal women were after her. The small, dark mark on the inside of her right elbow was attributed to the rope used by the tribe that captured her and the chronic scaly patch on her outside right wrist from a rope burn that did not heal. The ache in her shoulders came from exhaustion and hard labor, something she was not used to in that life. Her discomfort with swallowing was because Hardatha's throat was very dry, as she could not find much to drink while she was on the run. The scaly patch on her scalp was from a nervous habit that affected her when she was afraid. The tension behind her eyes was because it was, "hard to see how selfish I was."

Cecilia is married to Dale, whose past-life journey is chronicled in the next chapter. While they did not share the same lifetime, much of what she experienced as Hardatha will be echoed in her husband's Civil War life, most specifically their need to move to a home in the country. She explored this aspect when I asked if she had any bleed through about her life as Hardatha after our session.

"I recently moved to the Shenandoah Valley after living in a larger city most of my life," she explained. "After the regression I had a strong sense that I had come home to the mountains and I felt a great peace there. I was able to change my diet, which I had been unsuccessful in doing for some time. The "solar plexus" indigestion discomfort disappeared. I feel more comfortable in looking at myself in this life with more honesty."

In her initial questionnaire, Cecilia said her throat felt as if it were physically blocked so she was unable to speak in a loud, clear tone. That came up again in her regression when she described being tied to the post and left to die. She said, "I scream for help but no one comes." At the end of the regression, she said Hardatha's voice "was strong one minute and then gone the next." She added that her voice was swallowed by fear and that when she faces her fear, her voice comes back. That was echoed in her soul writing as well. I asked her to draw the parallel between that issue in Hardatha's life and in her own in terms of why this loss of voice would manifest again in this life.

"I have had a lot of experiences in this life that were difficult and where I felt powerless for things to be different," she explained. "As I have reclaimed my power, I find that sometimes I feel very strong and then can relapse into fear and want to be invisible again because it seems easier. Hardatha abused the power she had and then she became vulnerable and even though she had remorse, she died. Claiming one's power can feel very vulnerable at times and that is when the voice drops off. Awareness has helped me to understand what is happening and address the feelings."

As indicated earlier, Cecilia reported feeling a strong sense of indigestion around her solar plexus that showed up from time to time in this life, but then dissipated. When we did the regression and came to the scene of her evening meal, she was already on the run from the tribe's women who were chasing her with lethal intentions. When I asked about that evening meal, Cecilia said the indigestion pain "just showed up." She said Hardatha was eating a rabbit she had cooked over a fire and consumed quickly, glancing over her shoulder the entire time, afraid someone was going to come. Looking at the indigestion she occasionally felt in this life, and the indigestion described by Hardatha as she quickly ate on the run, I wondered if she saw any parallels between the two conditions in terms of why it would come up again in this life. What was its message?

"She was in great fear when this occurred," Cecilia explained. "I have noticed that it is not just about the food I eat, but the state of emotion I am in that seems to trigger the indigestion. Again, being aware of this link has, at least since the regression, made a difference as I have not experienced this symptom since then."

Hardatha admitted to using and manipulating people to the point of out and out cruelty with no remorse. I wondered if the behavior that Hardatha showed initially, followed by the karmic ramifications of that behavior, resonated with Cecilia in this life and if so, how were they manifesting in terms of the physical conditions she described.

"I have carried the sense in this life of over responsibility for everyone around me," Cecilia said. "Almost an apology for breathing. As I let go of that, fear can overtake me at times, like I'm not doing enough to make up for whatever I thought I did wrong in life. Fear leads to the loss of voice. Hardatha's life gives a sense of explanation of why I might feel that way because she is indeed responsible for causing others a lot of pain."

When trying to escape, Hardatha's horse is pulled down, resulting in her fall. In order to escape, Hardatha had to leave her horse in pain. As she told her story, I envisioned her ankle and foot getting caught in the rope that captured her horse, injuring her in the fall. The hip pain had to do with that fall as well. I could see where her current leg pain came from that fall and the hip pain from being dragged back once she was captured. I asked Cecilia if she felt those injuries represented anything in particular in terms of the message they conveyed to her in this life.

"I have had ankle and leg aches without any apparent injury that would come and go," she answered. "I felt like it was my body's way of getting my attention to something that I was not willing to look at."

Hardatha's death from cold and starvation has impacted Cecilia's intolerance of cold in this life. "In times when I am fearful, I have felt almost a compulsive need to be sure I have plenty to eat, more than I might actually need," she said. "Physically my muscles can feel very tight to the point of discomfort when I feel cold; more than what I think would be usual when I am in a heated building with warm clothes on.

Cecilia indicated that when Hardatha was captured, she begged to be free. She also begged for kindness—the same kindness she did not give to others. In this life, Cecilia said it was just the opposite—that she was "always trying to take care of people sometimes at the expense of myself." She wasn't sure if this tendency was a direct result of Hardatha's lack of empathy, but added, "it makes sense to me that that experience could carry over and manifest in that way—like trying to atone for lack of kindness in Hardatha."

Regardless of what we endured in a previous lifetime, it is how we respond that transmutes the karma. Cecilia was doing a very good job of that in this life and now with remembering details of Hardatha's life she could continue to resolve the karmic issues from that life and put them behind her once and for all. I asked Cecilia what that meant to her and she replied: "That I no longer have to carry the burden of trying to make up for that life. I can live now going forward with awareness of where that guilt came from and just live a good life now."

Cecilia reported that after the session, her physical condition did not go away completely, but improved substantially. "Increased awareness from this experience has shifted my life in seeming subtle ways but that feel bigger. While all symptoms did not go away, they seem manageable by the awareness."

Chapter Four

Weight & Digestive Issues

(Q) What is the cause of the body's dislike for eating fish, fowl, game and certain meats? (A) From the condition as existed in that as a Norseman, when he lived on these alone.

(Edgar Cayce Reading 5453-9).

By far, the physical karma that concerned the greatest number of volunteers had to do with weight and digestive issues. That's not surprising, considering how many possible causes there are for these issues.

Dr. Edith Fiore, a renowned past-life therapist and clinical psychologist, found that the eating disorders of many of her clients were connected to a past life. "I now find that almost all patients with chronic weight excess of ten pounds or more have had a lifetime in which they either starved to death or suffered food deprivation for long periods," she wrote. She added that this was especially prevalent in individuals who were part of native cultures and found themselves without food and water.

Edgar Cayce had much to say on physical karma dealing with this common malady. A reading for a 14-year-old boy revealed that his inclination toward digestive issues resulted from his indulgence in rich foods during his French and Persian incarnations.

Sometimes weight issues are rooted as much in past-life attitudes as in overindulgence or starvation. This was brought to light in a reading Cayce did for a 17-year-old female student who in a past life had made fun of people who were overweight. Now she struggled with her own weight and exercise issues.

In this chapter we will explore the past lives of three individuals who came to the project complaining of weight and digestive issues. Dale had issues stemming from a past life as a Civil War soldier, while Louise and Lee were dealing with the ramifications of lifetimes in England. We'll start with Dale, a 67-year-old retired lab manager who complained of irritable bowel syndrome.

It's Such a Damn Waste!

Dale was no stranger to past-life work and shared in vivid detail seven previous lives he knew about. Previous past-life work had given him insights into his current life motivations, fears and character traits and had greatly improved his spiritual outlook, ability to enjoy life and empathy for others. He wanted to continue his progress in personal growth so he took our session very seriously.

Dale's body-scan revealed tingling around his knees and left hip; discomfort in his left hip; and brought an awareness of a present-life injury to his right calf. He felt pressure in his urinary system and intestines and complained about his breathing. "I'd like to get more air than I usually get," he said. "It feels like a heaviness in my chest that impedes my breathing somewhat."

Continuing the scan, he said his inside right elbow had a small, dark mark. His right wrist had a chronic, scaly patch that comes and goes. He was aware of curvature of spine. When it came to scanning his shoulders, he remembered straining his shoulder muscle, although he could not feel it. He also remembered a football injury in high school to his right humerus.

His neck called to mind his difficulty with swallowing at times, saying his hyoid bone seemed to be displaced. He had braces on his teeth as a child and has had gum surgery, "they have been a weak spot." His nose was slightly stuffy and breathing felt constricted. There was a scaly patch on his scalp that came and went. He described tension around his eyes and said he had been near-sighted since 4th grade.

Dale was sure the irritable bowel syndrome came from his life as an African-American woman who was sold into slavery and died aboard ship, so he was very surprised when in our session a Civil War life popped up instead. He was born William Elliott around 1840 in North Carolina. William was a past-life aspect Dale was very familiar with. At the start of our session, Dale saw William as a barefoot 7-year-old boy wearing faded blue overalls and no shirt. He had light-colored fine hair that was "just trimmed every so often."

William lived on a farm in an area of gently rolling hills. He could see a farmhouse and barn, made of rough-hewn planks. The two-story house had a tin roof and a brick fireplace, with a rail on the front porch. At this point, Dale said his feet were "throbbing."

William ate his evening meal in a large dining room/ kitchen. He enjoyed chicken, mashed potatoes with gravy and spoon bread. He was using silverware and eating off plates that had a floral design in a circular pattern around the edge. "Not fine china, but it's chinaware and well used," he said.

Seated at the table were his parents, a younger and an older brother, and a sister. "They [parents] seem dark as if in a shadow," he said. He admitted being fearful of his father who was very stern. "I can see him (father) smacking the table with his fist. He's angry—we were laughing. He bangs the table with his fist. We got real quiet, real quick."

At this point, Dale became very emotional and began to weep, saying, "I want to go back to the barn to be with the cows and animals and away from my father." After this statement, he calmed down and returned to breathing deeply.

Dale recalled several significant events in William's life. The first occurred when he and his brothers were around a small fire pit. "It doesn't seem serious," he said. "Somebody stirred it up and embers got in our eyes."

William's father was standing near the fire and the boy could see his father's leg out of the corner of his eye. "Seemed like a huge oak tree," he said of his father's leg. "I'm just seeing his legs. He smacks me on the head. Seems like he's always angry. We caused a disturbance and he smacked me. My feet are throbbing—they want to go. I want to run up into the woods. There's a big rock—one of my favorite places to be. There's a creek there."

William did not go there after this incident with the fire pit, but said that was the place he'd like to go. "Just aware of need to run," he says. "I like to run. I like to be barefoot but I have to be careful so the cows don't step on my feet."

The next event William recalled was seeing his father firing a shotgun. "I think he's aiming at something. I feel like he would shoot me if I weren't careful. He's just so angry. My sister is there—she's a little younger than me. We were playing a game in the dirt. We're just little kids playing with sticks, digging holes."

William next describes going into his house. It is dark with the exception of a dim light coming from the fireplace. He is ten years old. "My father is angry. He throws something off the mantel. I feel like I want to be grown up enough to stand up to him. There is tightness in my body. I wish I were big enough to punch him and I am thinking one day I will be. One day I'm going to be big enough to. . . ." At this memory, Dale began to weep again.

The final event has William at age 16 saying he is not so much threatened by his father anymore. "I'm pitching hay. I like to do that. I like to be in the barn. I really like the cows."

Several years later he dies from a gunshot wound to the back during the battle at Gettysburg. He described the scene as confusing. "Gun smoke. I can't see anything. I don't want to be there. So confusing. I can't tell who is who. What am I doing here? Oh, God."

His last thoughts were, "It's such a damn waste." He looks down on the battlefield and sees his body alongside the body of a big chestnut horse that had also been shot and killed. Upon seeing the horse, Dale began to sob.

In examining similarities between William and Dale's lives, Dale said he had the same fearful father figure in this life, although the two fathers were different souls. Other similarities between Dale and William are their love of the outdoors, especially the woods, and animals. As for souls from that life in this life now, he identified his sister in this life as having been his sister in the previous life. "I was older in the previous life. She was older in this life. I tried to help her in that life and she tried to help me in this one." He recalled that in the previous life, his father had abused his sister and that memory caused him to weep again. Back to this life, he said his mother worked, "so his sister was caretaker and mother figure in many ways; a mentor."

Dale's Soul Writing

God, he abused my sister and I couldn't stop it. Why couldn't I stop it? . . ..[scribbles]. . . I like. . . there is a beauty in writing . . . [scribbles]. . . my hand wants to be free . . . [scribbles].

My Soul Writing

Look to the fear in that life as the source of the irritable bowel syndrome in this life. As a child William repeatedly felt a tightening in his stomach whenever his father was around. That tightening was from fear and from his own anger and frustration at his inability to alter his and his siblings' life. Having a fearful father in this life triggered that same reaction so he has had to contend with pain in the pit of his stomach ever since. Dale has learned that it is not merely brawn that enables one to escape an abusive situation, but thoughts can do as much. His escapism to nature helped to alleviate the pain. Unfortunately, his enlistment in the Confederate army, brought about as a means of escape, caused his early demise, but to the end he brought with him a love of animals that he feels today—his love for the horse was the last emotion he felt so that was so strong that it came in with him now. William's quest was always to be free. He equated that with running and being alone. For Dale it is the same quest, yet he finds other ways to achieve this—indicating soul's growth in this area. Dale has many pieces to William's life puzzle. It is for him to put it together and reveal the total picture—then and now."

Sometime after our session, Dale reported that he clearly could see how his intolerance for turmoil and loud noise has affected his relationships with family members, his wife, children, and grandchildren. "I have always sensed aggression in loud voices and have responded with unnecessary anger to children I perceive as unruly," he explained.

Since Dale had indicated he already was familiar with William's life, I asked him why he thought that life emerged again. He speculated that it had something to do with the fact that he and his wife had recently moved from an urban house in Richmond, Virginia to the less congested environment in the Shenandoah Valley.

During the regression, Dale discussed William's father as being physically abusive to his children and said he had smacked William on the head on numerous occasions. I asked Dale if he attributed that behavior to any physical karma he was dealing with today. He said he did not have a clear correlation between that behavior and the physical karma today, but wondered if it was related to tightness he sometimes felt in his forehead and the scaly patches on his scalp.

Similarly, William talked about his feet throbbing, that they wanted "to go." I asked Dale if there was a tie-in between what he said about his feet in William's life to what he was dealing with physically today.

"My lower body has disproportionately more strength than my upper body," he said. "In the experience as William Elliott, I wanted to be able to physically retaliate against my father but was not able to as a child. Running to the woods was my escape, so my feet and legs were my best asset, not my arm strength."

During the body scan, Dale mentioned his constricted breathing and pressure in his urinary system and intestines, both of which he easily could attribute to the tension in William's life.

When we discussed the scaly patches on his right wrist and scalp, he wondered if the scalp patches were related to William's father smacking him on the head, but he did not know for sure. A sign that they were connected was the fact that Dale reported those scaly patches began to reduce after the session and were continuing to do so months later.

Dale also saw a connection between his present shoulder discomfort and William's life. "I wonder if this is due to my upper body musculature not being very developed; a karmic result of William's not being able to strike out against his father," he said.

The difficulty he feels in swallowing is intensified by stress, which Dale could see in William's life, but added that it had not been an issue since our session.

Revisiting the regression, I reminded Dale that when William said he wanted to grow up enough to stand up to his father, it elicited great emotion. I asked if he could tie that feeling to where he felt it in his body in this life and he said he definitely felt it in his abdomen and his chest.

In reviewing William's short life Dale called it a "damn waste." I asked if that thought continued in this life and how did it appear in terms of the physical conditions he was experiencing in the here and now.

"My personality has tended to the depressive side," he explained. "At times I have dwelled on the waste of the wars that have occurred in this life, and my own confusion around the Vietnam War. I was in the Army during that war, but fortunately was stationed in the States. I certainly see a parallel with William's life and my current one; feeling forces controlled me I couldn't resist. This has led to periods of very low energy, and I have worked from nervous energy most of my life."

In the regression, William said his father had abused his sister and that William felt great guilt about not being able to stop that. That same theme came up in his soul writing. Dale indicated that William's sister is his sister in this life and that while his mother worked, his sister was his primary caretaker. I asked him to draw the parallels between the two life situations and to examine how that was showing up in his physical body. He reiterated what he said earlier, that it came in as low physical strength and abdominal tension from feeling he was caught in situations in which he had no control.

Fear is a prevalent emotion in past-life recall. Behind that fear can be found detailed accounts of a past-life trauma. I had a sense that the fear in William's life was the source of his irritable bowel syndrome in this life, as William had a tightening in his stomach whenever his father was around. That tightening not only was from fear, but also from his anger and frustration at his inability to alter his or his siblings' lives. Having a fearful father in this life triggered that same reaction. I asked if he believed that was an accurate assumption and if so, could he address that further.

Dale said in this life he became afraid of his father around the age of three and that this fear then transferred to fear of all authority figures, whether individuals or institutions. "During most of my life the world appeared to be a hostile place and I lived in nervous tension trying to navigate my way through the combat zone of life," he admitted.

William's quest always was to be free. William's escapism to nature helped to alleviate his pain. I asked Dale if he felt that was a true statement for then and for now, and he wholeheartedly agreed.

"As I stated, I lived most of my life seeing the world as a hostile environment in which I was constantly seeking safety and security. This extended to my concept of God as an impersonal force with no personal relation to me. This and other regression sessions have allowed me to experience the source of my fears, let my spirit exist through these lives and the deaths of these physical lives. Over time I have come to see lessons in these lives. One is that compassion and courage are contagious as are fear and anger."

I asked Dale to describe what the regression segment was like for him in terms of clarity of images, emotions and understanding, and further, how did his senses respond on all levels. He replied that aspects of the session were quite clear. While he was visually observing scenes in William's life, at the same time his other senses were providing information.

"I could see, hear and feel the family's cattle in the barn and smell the hay," he explained. "I could feel being struck on the head. I could feel my feet striking the ground as I ran to the woods. I could see the green woods and feel the soil. In anger at my father I could feel my arm muscles and fists tighten and I could feel constriction in my abdomen."

About a month after we met, Dale wrote to say that during the regression session, his first awareness was that of a 7-year-old child afraid of his angry father and wanting to run out of the house to the safety of the barn or the woods. About a week after the session, he awoke remembering his 7th year in his present life.

"Again I had an angry father who instilled fear and mistrust in me," Dale said. "My family had moved to a new neighborhood. As a scrawny newcomer, the other children picked on me in my new school. I learned to defend myself but kept to myself and had few friends. I retained this emotional aloofness throughout my adult life. I also carried a constant inner tension from a fear of not being accepted. I attribute my IBS to this tension."

Dale said the session positively impacted his life. "The session helped me see how my past-life pattern has carried into this life," he stated. "As a child in this life, I had a sense of safety and security at my grandmother's home, which was a very small, rustic farmhouse in a rural area. During visits there, I spent many hours in the farmyard and woods. As an adult I have had a desire to recreate this connection; wanting a house in the country, away from the pressures and irritations of urban life. At the same time, I am aware of the emotional cost of loneliness; of an isolated life avoiding the stresses of human relationships. Awareness has replaced the sadness I had over the loss of human connections over the years. Awareness has enabled me to grieve; my IBS continues to be more reduced. I can look at my new house, not as a cloistered retreat, but as a place from which to develop community involvement. Our session helped me realize that I still had unresolved anger about earlier life situations in which my responses were based on fear and led to regrets and resentments. The session has helped me clear them."

Dale said that his irritable bowel syndrome was not completely healed after the regression session, but it did improve substantially. Overall, he found the experience worthwhile.

"This and other sessions have shown me how fear and anger have reduced the quality of my life choices, reduced my ability to see options and opportunities and have affected my relationships," he said. "I practice much more positive thinking than I used to and continue to experience a growing faith in God as I now see lives as lessons, not random events or punishments."

Express Anger or Keep Eating It?

Louise is a 63-year old former marketing professional and self-described workaholic turned writer. She came to the session wanting to know the source of her low self-esteem and why she repressed herself with food. She knew it stemmed from previous lifetimes and was reinforced in her current life. She had been regressed previously to a past life in China in which she spoke out and as a result had her tongue cut out and left in a hut in a dusty barren countryside to die. As she lay face down in the dirt, she contemplated eating an insect, knowing that could be her last meal. Her last thought in that life was, "fat people live longer." She realized that for someone like her, who had dedicated her life to being on a spiritual journey, the relationship between spirit and body was a source of learning and mastery.

During the body scan, Louise described a great deal of emotion in her thighs and hips, adding, "under that the true legs are giraffe, knobby knees." She had been ridiculed for knobby knees and her hips used to be a source of teasing. "I didn't understand it was for fun," she said.

When scanning her stomach, Louise felt agitation, but added that she was doing a cleansing that day. "Digestion is where I process life," she said.

Looking at her hands and arms, she described a scar on her left thumb from a bout of measles when she was baby, and a circular scar on her left arm from immunization.

Her spine was slightly swayed back. When she scanned her shoulders she said there was an "echo of being attacked as a baby in my left shoulder. It's been released but my body is reminding me of the hands of my older sister—a continual echo of fear of being unprotected."

She reported seeing a circle, perhaps a chakra, on her neck. A bear appeared in her mind's eye and asked what her goals were, i.e. "Are you going to express your anger or keep eating it?" Scanning her head she found laughter and a spiritual connection came over her when I asked her to scan her pineal gland. In examining her head, she remarked that her eyes are too close together.

After the scan, Louise's soul took her back to a life in 1792 in Canterbury, England where she saw herself as a 47-year-old woman named Elizabeth. When asked if she could identify a last name, she said it was Elizabeth "of something," referring to the name of her duchy.

Elizabeth had pasty, pale skin and her hands were "wussy, delicate, soft, refined" and well cared for. She had brown hair worn curly around her face, but straight when tightly pulled back. She had on a blue dress made of a shimmery, shining fabric, possibly satin, and shoes she said were elegant and expensive.

She described herself as a stalwart woman of intention, "not like 'don't mess with me' but more 'I know what I'm doing.'" She was knowledgeable, aware and intelligent. She claimed to be British royalty and was in the center of government and power, i.e., "wearing power in a royalty sense."

She lived in a rolling, lush, green countryside dotted with trees and stone walls that divided the pastures and fields into geometric patterns. She called it, "a typical English countryside."

Elizabeth found herself on the first floor landing of a castle-like structure with Palladian windows and a stairway that led upward into total darkness. The castle was strong, with pointed arches and cathedral-like architecture of high ceilings, rich gilding and an abundance of white marble. She described it as, "sumptuous, rich, iconic—something that stands for something." She was dedicated and dutiful to that grand place. It was her position and she was true to it.

Elizabeth took her evening meal in one of several dining rooms. She sat at a trestle-type, wood table with turned legs, and balls at the foot of the legs. The table was adorned with silver utensils, goblets and silver candelabra. The meal consisted of fresh, green vegetables that were moist and tasty. She saw herself in two different eating areas; sometimes eating from a common pewter plate in the scullery kitchen; sometimes eating off of white china adorned with pink flowers and gold around the fancy-edged rim that contained crests. She ate alone, "as if I had a public day with visitors and am in a retreat."

When she focused on the significant event in that life, she described different surroundings consisting of rounded stone archways, a stone wall behind her and darkness in the building. She believed she was some place further out in the country, away from the castle.

"I'm in front of crowds of people," she recalled. "There is a hanging or a beheading—something going on. Am I the cause of it or am I stopping it? I think I'm saying no. I think I'm being stalwart; standing my ground. A woman is screaming; demanding something. She's the rabble-rouser. The crowd got quiet and shrank upon itself. The energy shriveled down until there was nothing there. I refused to engage. I don't know what they wanted but they didn't get it this time. Maybe the kingdom is becoming unhappy. Maybe there's political strife. It was a warning to me—change is coming. Maybe that was the last time they listened to me. Maybe no matter how honorably a role is executed it is powerless when its time is over. I appear to be resolute but I turn around and walk inside in somewhat of a petulant snit. The way you leave a gathering is significant. I usually don't leave. The visitors leave when their short time with me is over. In this case, I turned my back on the crowd and went back inside. They rattled me. They angered me. Frustrated and disappointed me. Left me thinking, 'what do I do with this?' I was refined. I wanted the people to learn to be refined, to live by higher thought processes, but they were just ordinary. I embodied it. I was kind. I listened. I was open. I honored people who came to visit me. I heard their point of view of what they were wanting. I wanted the people to behave as if they were royalty, too; to bestow themselves with this sense of honor, but they couldn't. I could not change them—you cannot do that. Their lives were different from mine so why would they think like I do? So in this life I still find it difficult to be with people who say I want more from you. 'Look at me suffering. You have to suffer to know me.' I don't need to suffer with them. My digestion keeps trying to process the inequities. My siblings [in this life] make their fist at me—'how dare you be happy when I have such difficulties and have such a hard time.' 'I am so depressed,' they say, and I want to kick their ass."

She next saw herself standing in a parlor facing a bank of windows. There had been visitors that day, but they had left. A woman in a turquoise dress, whom Louise described as her mother in this life and who wore that same dress to Louise's wedding, walks into the parlor and holds a knife to Elizabeth's back.

"I am unprotected in my own home," Elizabeth said. Louise later realized she felt that same way in her childhood home. Returning to Elizabeth's voice, she says: "I see one of two common farmer women shrouded in a dull, dark cloth who were allowed in. While my mother [in this life] holds a knife to my back, one of the other women knifes me in the stomach."

Elizabeth's last thoughts were of betrayal—"No gratitude for me. Anger. I'm spinning right now." In terms of unfinished business, she said, " I failed to make people happy. It's not possible."

When asked if she saw any parallels between Elizabeth's life and hers, Louise said: "I'm happy and I like to share happiness, express it, enjoy my humor and light heartedness, especially as I reveal it more, become one with it myself. My family destroyed me in this life—no protection—I was the scapegoat. I gagged on food when I was singled out at the dinner table. I took all the ranting and raving. By the time I was a teen, I knew no one cared what I felt, said or did—to be made fun of, derided, mocked, that as a person I didn't exist. It never occurred to me to actually speak up for myself lest worse consequences occur and because the experience of having a knife held in my back remained, I dared not make a move. They all did a good job if it was karmic. When you don't know that you are a spirit in a body and when you think that what you are is your thoughts, your feelings, or your body, others can take away your identity through their own aggressive behavior. They did a good job of destroying my confidence. Elizabeth had some innocence and bright light. She was a good person, inspiring, but people turned on her."

Louise's Soul Writing

Of course some things you did made some unhappy, but that's the way it is, my dear. Do not be blinded by your own purity and assume others are the same. Humans can do anything! You are less human and more spirit, but to live among the humans you must learn their ways. They are capable of this atrocity! Yes! Learn of dedication, being there to another, turning on the one, betraying the one. Rarely can you trust someone always. Learn to see with wise eyes and a knowing sensibility. You adapt and adjust like the flow of water does—this is your great achievement. But know others may not be willing or able. Spirit will protect you always in accordance with your purpose and need to learn something. Continue to speak up for yourself and know the reactions around you may be unpredictable. All people are at choice always. You only need to express yourself for yourself. Keep flowing. The pen is your sword. Wield it until the day you die. It is an endless flow of beauty for humanity. Allow yourself to flow with opportunities rather than the desire to push the river. Bob enjoyably, bubbling and gurgling along with the river. These repeating souls are teaching you human behavior. They allow no unintended harm to come to you—only the intended lesson.

My Soul Writing

. . . The weight issue for her is the same for many souls having an emptiness inside that needs to be filled with love. An insatiable appetite for love—the one thing withheld or not given enough of. That hole needs filling and so food acts as a temporary fix—feeling

full and whole when ingested. Louise has moved beyond this now,
although remnants remain for her to heal and resolve. Her work
with others will do that . . . .

As a shamanic healer well skilled in past-life healing, Louise was able to identify much of the residual effects of her previous life with what she was dealing with now and could trace the discomfort she identified in the body scan with what transpired in her regression.

For instance, when I reminded her that she indicated she felt "emotion" in her thighs and hips, she attributed that to frustration and nervousness being around her present family. The agitation in her stomach was tied to the knife that she was about to process out after learning about Elizabeth's death.

She associated the "eyes close together" with the crow totem, i.e. "Looking at life straight on and then looking at it from the side—like a shaman. Elizabeth was wise but not smart like the crow yet."

Louise experienced a great deal of bleed through after our session and actually sent me 12 pages of insights and thoughts to demonstrate one way her past life could be healed. "This was a significant past life that releases my family members and some others from karmic behavior in this lifetime, as I master the lesson now following the past-life regression," she said.

During the body scan, Louise indicated agitation in her stomach area, adding that, "Digestion is where I process life." In the regression, Elizabeth said, "My digestion keeps trying to process the inequities." I asked if digestion is where she processes life and inequity, how did that fit in with her weight issues, and more importantly, how did she connect it to Elizabeth's life?

"One obvious answer to this question is the knifing in the gut," she said. "Energetically, the knife is the energetic layer up for healing. Turmoil in the countryside equals turmoil in the gut. Betrayal of my staff and supporters, hatred for my ways, jealousy of my blessings is all on the hand of the knife. My naiveté about connecting with people is my lesson. People are capable of anything. Hatred is real. Being hated hurts, when you receive it into your gut."

Louise described Elizabeth as very self-assured, knowing who she was and what she was all about. Yet in her initial questionnaire, Louise said she wanted to explore a past life to find the origin of her low self-esteem. In that regard, it appeared she and Elizabeth were at opposite ends of the spectrum. I asked her to tie this together and explain how it has manifested in a physical condition for her.

"The murder of confident, blissful Elizabeth was the taking of her self-esteem," Louise explained. "She gave it to the knife and to the raucous crowd—betrayers all! She ran. She fled. She left her body and watched from the arched ceiling above as the murder was completed and the looting of the castle occurred. In self-evaluation, she was a good person doing good deeds, sharing her wealth and love. She loved the castle as people love their pets and families. Inviting people in was a magnanimous gesture, wanting to share it with others. She was a weak leader or icon, not endowed with a threatening, strong quality and part of a crumbling ruling family. After her, then who? Why wait? Just get rid of her now! Her responses to the raucous crowd were surprise, being stunned and frozen and thinking, 'How dare they?' Being nice isn't enough. To her, being nice was everything."

Elizabeth said the crowd rattled her, angered her, frustrated and disappointed her to the point where she was left thinking,

"What do I do with this?" I asked Louise whether those feelings resonated to her in this life and if so, how were they manifesting in terms of her physical condition?

Louise admitted that from her earliest memories in this life, she has had the same thought as Elizabeth, i.e., "What do I do with this?" and "How dare they? How can they? How could she?" Important issues were never discussed. Her mother kept a shiny clean house and the house was prepared for her father's "reign" on the weekend and then cleaned up afterwards. In essence, everything was swept under the rug. On the surface everything appeared to be clean, but that was only a ruse to hide the truth underneath. It was a very two-faced existence.

"The anger of frustration and hatred grew in me," she said. "Defiance, petulance hidden inside my smiling face, athletic body, and mercurial energy. Finally the day came when out of anger I started to imitate my father so he would see the anger he sent out at me and how he would eat sugar to salve his seething soul. I would imitate him. 'Oh, woe is me. I got on the scale this morning and gained a pound! Oh, how did that happen? I have no idea! Life is difficult!' When I sweep my anger or the anger of others around me under the carpet, so to speak, by eating it, eventually the carpet starts to bulge! What do I do with this? I eat it. No self-esteem to stop me. Enough anger to keep it up, unchecked for years."

Another recurrent theme in Elizabeth's life was honor. Once again, I asked Louise if that sentiment resonated to her in this life and if so, how was it surfacing in terms of the physical conditions she was experiencing.

"Compassion and naiveté equal disaster," she said. "I am continually amazed what people will do or say, even in my own home. In this lifetime, it determines who gets invited in and who does not. I have learned that what people say and do are reflections on them, not on me, but still it is a determining factor. As my self-esteem and self-respect have grown in this lifetime, so has my discernment about others and their roles in my life."

Elizabeth was annoyed with the people around her and Louise indicated her annoyance with her siblings. "I want to kick their ass," she said of the latter group. I asked her to draw the parallel between Elizabeth's annoyance with her people and her annoyance with her siblings and discuss, if relevant, how that is manifesting in the weight issues she brought up.

"I was alone in a family of six," she said. "There were no sisterly moments or brotherly love; a great wasteland of emptiness developed where joy and love could have grown."

Another theme in Louise's session was protection. When Elizabeth was killed, she said, "I am unprotected in my own home, as in this life, no protection." Later Louise said her current family destroyed her in this life—"no protection, I was the scapegoat." She also said, "I gagged on food because I was being yelled at."

Considering Elizabeth's fatal wound is in her stomach area, I asked Louise if she could see the connection and how it has manifested as a weight issue in this life.

"My family members never came to my rescue from the verbal abuse I withstood in their presence," she admitted. "It was never mentioned, as if it never happened. I saw them, particularly my mother, as betrayers as much as my dad. I had no one to lean on; nowhere to go for resolution, and was unable to vocalize the situation—to even know that it was not normal. I knew in my gut it was wrong. My face took on the embarrassment, my throat the choking. It was at the dinner table where dad was so brutal to me. Since Elizabeth was knifed shortly after her meal, I must have internalized the idea that, "If I'm still eating, it wasn't time to be knifed. I could postpone the inevitable."

Many individuals who experience weight issues in this life report feeling empty inside. That hole needed filling so food acted as a temporary fix. Louise agreed that was an accurate description of her situation.

"I blamed my family for creating the emptiness inside me all throughout my poor boohooing days until I realized that it is up to me to fill the void with love," she said. "Now I have the opportunity to choose to fill it with self-love instead of food. In the end, God may say, 'all those selfless acts of kindness are interesting, but how much did you love yourself?' It just could be all about self-love."

Of the soul-writing session, Louise called it "easy and comfortable," adding that because the lesson being taught to Elizabeth was a tough one, "it was comforting to have guidance that points out I have been protected except for the actual lesson needed. I gained perspective in the soul writing that I had many rich and valuable experiences growing up in this life and that the suffering that occurred was specific to the actual lesson needed."

The regression and soul-writing session is enabling her to find deeper clarity where eating has caused so much confusion and fogginess for her. "If I can accept that others can have anger, hatred and tantrums, then I can be at ease and comfortable and not need to eat it away." She is also learning to express her own anger and to strengthen her personal boundaries.

As someone who delves into past lives with her own clients, I asked Louise how much more valuable was our session by adding the soul-writing aspect. "Oh, I think that is marvelous," she said. "It allows us to consciously connect with Spirit and receive guidance with our eyes open in this world in this lifetime, which helps to bring us back to the present moment. Writing is a way to heal!"

Louise concluded by saying that while her eating habits did not change completely, they have improved substantially.

"My awareness and clarity on eating increased, my mental and emotional understanding of the behavior increased, and energetically, I gathered up Elizabeth's aspect of my being, removed the knife, and made peace with the lesson. If the pounds start to drop off, I will let you know! I definitely have noticed that I am not turning to food like before. I will say this: I have joined a gym and a swimsuit arrived in the mail yesterday! Looks like I'm serious about loving my body!"

We Are Not in This Alone

Sixty-three year-old Lee came to the project seeking answers about the source of her Crohn's disease. During the body scan, she felt something in her stomach, describing it as a "big stone, emptiness, and heavy weight in digestive system." She was nauseous and also felt something on her left side. Her heart was racing "like butterfly wings—not normal," she said. "Things are moving too fast. I almost can't catch my breath."

Lee's regression took her back to 1139 in England where she saw herself as a 20-year-old, healthy, tan male with long, curly blonde hair. His name was Yohanson, but his wife called him Yon. He wore brown leather sandals that had several straps to hold them in place. His clean, but well-worn, clothing consisted of a rough burlap tunic top, short skirt, and belt with a knife hanging from it.

Yon was outside walking next to his ox cart. He described the landscape as having golden fields and gentle hills. It was a hot, sunny fall day and he could smell the sun on the crops. He lived on a farm out in the country, but a town could be seen in the distance. His dark taupe adobe house had small windows. Both the house and barn were low to the ground and connected to each other. The buildings had a high-pitched roof, but the walls were only four feet high so upon entering you had to duck before you could stand upright. Yon called the house attractive and said it made him feel good.

The evening meal consisted of "mushy" beef stew, potatoes, carrots and onions that had been re-cooked multiple times. Yon spooned the food out of a wooden bowl. He described much laughter and ease at the table, which he shared with his wife, their 6-year-old curly-haired daughter, 4-year-old son, an infant son sitting in a "funny chair" at the table, and his mother. He described his wife as having long dark hair, with a great smile and beautiful teeth. "To have a happy wife—that is a blessing," he said. "To have smiles and laughter—that's rare. To come home and be happy—that's good. Most don't have that at all."

His 40-year old mother—considered old for that time— lived with them. He described her as gray-haired with a shawl over her head. She wore an "all encompassing apron over a brown dress." Missing were his two brothers who left to fight in the Crusades. Yon opted to remain behind to tend to the family farm and was proud that he made such a smart decision. "I don't believe in Christianity—that's why I'm smart!" he said with pride. "They went to fight for something that's not real. That's my mother's sadness—that I don't believe and she's given two sons to it. I gave her the gift of this healthy farm."

Yon's significant event was his death at the age of 22. He was working in the pasture close to the barn, putting in a post for a gate and fence. "I was speared by a tree post that had been cut to put in the ground and it's run through me," he said. "It was an accident. It fell off. There were ropes to leverage it up. I'm working alone. I rigged this to lift it up to put it in the hole and it slipped. It came through me. That is my death."

When asked about his last thoughts as his soul left his body, Yon replied, "My arrogance that I could do it alone and that I was leaving my family and they couldn't survive without me. It was a two-man job and I knew it. I felt I could do anything. I'm me. The arrogance is amazing, amazing, overwhelming. I really had a strong sense of how right, smart, good I am—how lucky my wife was to have me. How my mother should know and realize how lucky she is that I took care of the farm."

In terms of unfinished business, Yon said, "I should have raised my children. I should have heard my mother say 'thank you' and acknowledge my good care of the farm. My memory of others was dark and not good."

Yon said his wife's brothers came and cared for the farm after his death. While he was "okay" with that, he thought no one could do it as wonderfully as he. "God, what an ego!" Lee laughed.

Lee had a revelation at this point. "I think Yon's blondeness is unique," she said. "I think he has a different heritage from these people. He was born there. That was his home. But I get the sense he is an outsider because of his long gone father. His two brothers were older. His sisters had married and went to other farms. Yon's father was from the northern country. I'm getting the word 'invasion.' He was assigned to this area to monitor something. Very much smarter—very much—different ideas from these 'commoners.' I'm thinking Vikings, making wooden ships, technique for leverage. Yon's mother was a commoner. [She was] made to feel less than. The sons who went on to the Crusades were her favorites, whereas Yon was his father's child."

Lee admitted to sharing Yon's arrogant attitude that she could do it alone. "I could take care of my late husband and it almost killed me. I could do it. He could count on me. Not going for help or asking for others—that you do your own misery quietly, you eat it. Yon was on top, king of the heap." Her final comments on that life were: "It was a very good life. We are not in this alone."

Lee's Soul Writing

. . . Lee our joy, our beauty, you were so full of yourself, a gift from the then father. How strong and able and smart and like his people you were. This you took in, as an all-encompassing ability so there was no room for God and Godliness. This was the downfall. To scorn your mother's life of Godliness and your brothers' need to make manifest their truths. Your arrogance was your downfall. Not asking for help from others or God. Not allowing your world to be bigger than you! You have now learned the importance of others. You let your husband go before he died and that was/is key. Your illness is not needed now. You have learned your lessons. It is not up to you to carry those around you. It is up to you to bring them joy and laughter and love, to give them a place of calm and shelter but not to carry them. . .

While Lee did not experience any bleed through from the regression, she admitted that she had given a lot of thought to the revenge aspect and how responsible one can be for things that happened in another lifetime.

Reviewing her body scan, I noted that she had described a "big stone, emptiness, and heavy weight in the digestive system." She also described feeling nauseous and that there was something on her left side. She attributed that to the Crohn's disease. "When having a Crohn's attack, it is most often on the left side," she explained. "In fact, that is where they most frequently cut out the diseased parts."

She also indicated problems in her chest, complaining her heart was racing like butterfly wings. When she said things were moving too fast that she almost could not catch her breath, I asked if she meant that literally or figuratively; if the heart palpitations had anything to do with what Yon experienced in his life. She said it did.

"The knowledge that he was dying would have caused heart distress, but it also could have been from a loss of blood or other physical problem related to being speared with a log."

Lee made it a point several times to describe the happiness and joy that existed in that lifetime. Rather than bringing that with her in this life, Lee designed her current life to be the complete opposite.

"In fact, married life with my husband, who was one of the brothers sent off to die in the Crusades, was quite the opposite," she admitted. "He got so bad that we were not allowed to talk at the Thanksgiving table, nor was I allowed to laugh in the house. Our kids were not allowed to have their friends in the house, because they were too noisy laughing and playing. In the family where I grew up, there were seven children, and it also was not a happy household. My mother was probably bipolar and not a happy person at all. We kids had to be very sensitive to her moods to stay out of her way, so the overall feeling was one of wariness."

Another theme in Yon's life was his need to be acknowledged for what he did. I asked how that related to her present life and physical condition.

"I could never do anything right in my mother's eyes," Lee said. "She and my step-father were always supportive of the boys and the girls were not worth anything. I did very well in business and would make the joke that it never would have occurred to my mother that I would be in business; therefore she never got a chance to say how badly I would do. My husband also was like that."

Similar to his need for acknowledgment, Yon's arrogance was evidenced by his statement: "My thought is no one can do it as wonderfully as me," or, "How lucky my wife was to have me." His inability to ask for help led to his death. Lee admitted to sharing his attitude that you can do it alone and she referenced her care of her husband as an example. She said: "Not going for help or asking for others—that you do your own misery quietly, you eat it." I asked if she saw a correlation with that statement and her Crohn's disease.

"Most definitely," she replied. "In fact, it was the doctors who took my husband out of our home and put him in a nursing home. I would never have had the courage to do that on my own. It was not that he was not doing well; it was that it became so obvious that the family (the kids and I) were not doing well. In fact, I had a serious operation for the Crohn's after three years of caring for him at home. I almost died and was in the hospital for over a month while my mother took care of my husband and the kids. Not a good situation and caused me considerable stress. I have since adapted my view on this. I am more than willing to ask for help in all manner of things, recognizing that it gives others a chance to be helpful. God's angels come in all shapes and sizes. I am very willing to let them practice on me."

Another theme was Yon's lack of a spiritual background. In relation to his brothers marching off to the Crusades and his staying behind, he said: "I don't believe in Christianity—that's why I'm smart!" Yon also indicated that his mother favored his brothers because they did go off to fight, "for something that's not real." I asked Lee whether that theme still existed in her life today and from her response, nothing had changed in that regard.

"I am strongly against the idea of organized religion—religion as a business, giving away one's spiritual connection to God by dealing with a 'man of the cloth.' Being taught obvious untruths that are passed off as the word of God, even though most people know that the Bible has been rewritten by men with various agendas a number of times and the forgotten or hidden books of the Bible continue to be left out of formal discussions. I consider my relationship with God to be one of the most important things a person can have and to give that up is unthinkable. Although I do understand that people can feel the need to have a 'teacher' or a guide in this relationship, I cannot understand anyone giving up their own personal, intellectual power for this."

One of the other issues that came up during Lee's regression was that Yon had a different father and therefore looked different than his siblings and often felt like an outsider, referring to his brothers as "commoners." I asked how being different factored into her life today.

"I feel very strongly that there is an evolutionary imperative to the universe," she said. "It is funny, but I have never felt like I have been a part of any of the groups that I have found myself in. Being an unwanted girl in a large family of five boys and on through school experiences, I always have felt like an outsider. I used to hope I was adopted and someone would come and claim me, or that I had an adopted out brother who would come into the family and recognize me as his family. I also felt glad that my mother-in-law died before I met my husband, so I did not have to deal with her. I think he married me, in part, to irritate his family because I was so obviously a northerner—a brash, outspoken woman who would not hold her peace and had no respect for the southern way. It can get stressful, feeling or knowing you are the only one—that there is no one else on your team."

In Lee's soul writing, her Source wrote that she had learned her lessons. I asked whether she considered that a true statement.

"As I get older, I am definitely wiser," she said. "I can honestly say I am willing to let everyone make their own mistakes. I still can be shocked and disconcerted and amused by their stupidity, but I am no longer responsible for anyone but myself. My arrogance is now limited to myself and trying to choose what is best at this stage of my life for me. I find it unthinkable that I would talk someone into doing anything. I do feel like I have suffered through one hundred lifetimes with my husband. He has exerted his power over me and repeatedly ruined my family life in many, many lifetimes, even to the extent of killing the kids. I have paid him back with grace in this lifetime by trying to give him a loving family and taking care of him until it was no longer allowed."

Also in her soul writing, she was told it was up to her to bring joy, laughter and love, playing off the statements Yon made about his happy home. I asked how that correlated with her present life.

"I always have been the one to plan the large family gatherings by coercing everyone to go up to Maine for a weekend or longer to visit with the folks," Lee said. "I am sure that without me planning these gatherings and harping on everyone, my parents would have had very limited access to all their grandkids because no one would have gone to visit them. Since my husband was a horrible father and spouse, what happiness we had in my own home was created by me—any trips, adventures and good times. The family was my responsibility. These were my kids. My husband had said as much. I guess now that my kids are adults, I can release myself from that burden. Their happiness is their own responsibility. Although I think Yon felt that the fact that he made the farm productive and that he had married a happy woman and brought her to the farm was the reason that he deserved the credit for the happiness of the family. He could not imagine the family without him."

The cause of death from the spearing was significant because my soul writing subsequently revealed that it became the instrument of death for Yon's two brothers. One of those brothers became her husband in this life, thus the physical symptoms in this life were aggravated by her husband's presence. I asked Lee what that meant to her and she said she found it "right on!" She went on to say that exactly one year after they were married, she had her first Crohn's-related operation. "His disdain of me was palatable and I could never understand what happened to the loving, doting fiancé who changed overnight to the husband I lived with."

I asked Lee if the location of the fatal wound from Yon's life had anything in common with her present malady and she said while there were no birthmarks where the spear entered his side, she still has pain in that exact spot whenever she has a Crohn's attack.

Lee said that this was a remarkably clear regression for her. "The fields were so vibrant; the colors of the hay, the smells, my own happiness was very real. In fact, these feelings of happiness and well being are not something that I have often felt in this lifetime. That connectedness with all things, that 'all is right with the world' was a very strong and wonderfully pleasant feeling."

As with most other volunteers for this project, Lee had no idea about the lifetime she visited. She had done soul writing before so this was not new for her. "I think I am lucky that I can do this writing 'on demand as it were,' she said. "It seems my angels are always ready to talk to me and are just waiting for me to ask them in." She added that this soul-writing session gave her confirmation that her relationship with the soul that was her husband was over and that she is finally free.

"I have been struck with thinking about the burden of revenge," she said. "The ability of one person to curse another, to have so much negative energy directed at a person that it flows from lifetime to lifetime. The grip that hate and evil have, and how I do not want to be a part of it at all and how now I have paid my dues and it is over."

The best news of all from this session is that Lee reported that all of her symptoms disappeared, resulting in a spontaneous healing. "I feel strongly that I am in remission from the Crohn's disease," she said. "I feel more than a little hopeful that it will no longer be plaguing me—that I have outdistanced it for whatever reason, and for that, I am so grateful!"

Chapter Five

Liver & Kidneys

"God measures out affliction to our need."
—St. John Chrysostom: Homily IV

In 1942, the parents of an 11-year-old boy contacted Edgar Cayce for answers as to the cause of their son's bedwetting. This started when he was two and learned a sibling would join him. The parents thought he was reverting to baby habits so he wouldn't feel replaced. He was put under psychiatric care until he was four, and again from the ages of 8-10, but the condition persisted. Cayce said this was the result, "not merely a physical condition, but it reverts to the disturbance the entity brought to others because of their beliefs, faiths or activities" (2779-1).

Cayce said in a past life the boy had been a minister who condemned children to "ducking" because of their ability to see, hear or experience voices from other realms. Now he was the one experiencing the "ducking" through bedwetting.

The two research subjects outlined in this chapter have fascinating stories that explain the origin of their chronic liver and kidney conditions.

I am all I need

Anila is a 34-year-old stay-at-home mom and doula. She was an interesting subject in that she clearly remembered experiencing nearly identical issues in past lives taking place in 1311 and 1675. In both lives, she loved the soul of someone who is in her current life as well, and in both lives she was killed as a result of her search for him. I knew nothing about the 1311 life, but had regressed her earlier to the 1675 life where she was a 22-year-old Native American girl living in what would become southern Montana. That life ended when her lover's mother inserted a long thin needle into her back and punctured her liver. Anila felt her current liver problems surfaced once she reunited with her lost love again in this life.

"I have had pain on my right side in the back and front along my ribs that has increased over the past few months, and increased more after a healing session with a practitioner I now know to be my reincarnated love," she said. "There is a point where I have chronic ache and sometimes muscle cramps (where the needle was inserted and the point came through in 1675). I also have a liver qi deficiency I am working on with a naturopath."

Since 22—the same age she was in the 1675 life—she has had feelings of loneliness, despair, and being emotionally overwhelmed. She has had bouts of anger and suppressed emotions that she believes has resulted in the liver qi deficiency.

During her body scan, she noted a mole on her right big toe and reported having problems with bone spurs in her heels. She described an ache in her right knee and back upper part of her calf. There was a mole on her left hipbone above the pelvic bone and tightness in her hips. She described an aching feeling above her pelvic bone and described a scar from a rupture from an ectopic pregnancy, as well as ovarian cysts. She had considerable discomfort on her left side. She also had a mole inside her navel. Not surprisingly, she said the area around her liver ached and described pain in the farthest upper left corner of her stomach. She experienced muscle spasms on the right side of her abdominal wall and said when she was younger, the left side of her abdomen, from her liver down her rib cage, was lighter in color. She described a spot on her chest along the right side of her sternum that aches and cracks a lot. There is a mole under her left arm and a birthmark on the pointer finger of her left hand between her palm and second knuckle and in the same place on her pinky finger. She described an ache in her sacrum between her hips and said she has a mole on her spine above the shoulder line. There is a spot on her shoulders and another mole on each side of her neck around the collarbone where her shoulders connect to her arms. Her thyroid is sometimes swollen and she has a birthmark at the center of her forehead where it connects to the hairline. The middle back part of her scalp tingles a lot and that is where she loses a lot of hair. She also has a mole on her scalp in the center of her head.

When we started the session, we thought we were going to explore her life in 1311, thinking this was the origin of her liver problems, but when I led her to the door leading to the life in which her chronic condition began, the door marked 1311 was locked. I switched to a different guided imagery, but again she was unable to see anything, saying she "felt blind." Finally on our third attempt, she saw herself in 800 B.C. in Mesopotamia and we quickly realized this earlier life was the true source of her current chronic condition.

It was here that Anila recognized her past-life aspect, this time a male named Kaoolct Maomae. He was of average height, stout, with calloused hands. His skin was very dark and he looked older than his 17 years. He wore a belted, one-piece garment that looked like a dress and went to the knee. He had on makeshift sandals made of animal skin. His hair was very dark, almost black. It was coarse, with just a patch of it at the back of the top of his head fashioned in a loop with a bone through it. His forehead was adorned with ceremonial paint. He was at an outdoor wedding ceremonial site. He ate nothing, but was given a fermented drink. He knew the people around him, including the medicine man overseeing the ceremony. His pre-teen bride was a slender and pretty girl. They were entering marriage freely, but with some trepidation.

"She was going to be sent away as a peace offering to an older man from a different village, but the medicine man has bad intentions and wants power," Kaoolct says. "We don't want to be separated so we agree to be married. The medicine man wants war and knows this will cause problems."

And that's exactly what happened. "There was fighting after the wedding and we lost," Kaoolct says. "He [elder from the other tribe] doesn't want her now because she is married, but someone has to pay. He was going to kill her but says he'll take me as a slave—and other things like supplies—to pay for breaking the agreement. That is the condition for peace. My arms are stretched out and bound to the ends of a branch they placed over my shoulders. I have to walk. Sometimes they drag me. I try to escape once we're there. They put me back on the rack. Sometimes they just keep my hands tied behind my back. Life is bad there but I have a very strong will. The elder wants me to be able to work but not run. He damages my right knee and my right foot. He smashes my toes so I limp. He takes pieces of my skin under my left arm and wears them as a trophy. He wants to break me but I have a strong heart. I picture her when I need to escape the suffering."

Kaoolct meets the young son of the elder who is kind to him. "He sometimes brings me things to put on sores, and water," he said. "Now that I can't run and am weak they only bind me at night. Sometimes above the elbows and wrists, arms behind my back."

He remains in captivity for nearly six years. The young boy now is grown and is a healer. "He's very good at what he does and is very smart," Kaoolct says. "I love him like he's my son. For a long time the elder was unaware of the bond between us. He sees that now and is angry with me. He is too prideful. He'll teach his son a lesson. He punishes me by tying me to a stake again. I have to kneel for a long time. He hits me. I'm ready to leave. I'm almost dead."

Kaoolct remains bound for several days with his wrists tied to his feet. "I've fallen over to my side. I was dreaming of her and things we did together. It's cool and dark outside. I'm bleeding inside I think. The boy comes to say goodbye."

Kaoolct dies at the age of 25 but he feels much older. "My body is very tired," he says. The boy gives poison to Kaoolct to hasten his death. "He dips something and sticks it into a wound above my heart." The boy stays with Kaoolct until he passes.

Kaoolct's last thoughts are of his young wife and of having another chance for a real life. "Thinking I must always be strong. Live from the heart when necessary. That sometimes with great sacrifice also comes great gifts and wondering if I'll ever have the chance again to watch over that boy."

Anila said that like Kaoolct, she is very strong willed. "I have a very big heart," she said. "I have closed it off for a long time until recently. I sacrifice for those I love, sometimes to the point of my own suffering. This lifetime (800 B.C.) started the pattern. It was the first time I died for that soul."

When asked if any of the souls from that life were in her life now, Anila said the young girl who was married to Kaoolct is a friend of hers now, but did not identify her. The boy incarnated as the mother in the 1675 lifetime and is again in Anila's current life in the role of her meditation teacher. The elder who mistreated Kaoolct is her mother-in-law.

"I don't see or speak to her anymore," Anila said of her mother-in-law. "She hates me. All the good she sees in me she doesn't see in herself. Alcoholic, filled with venom and anger, and takes it out on me. I knew the moment I met her I was everything she'd never be in her mind. Everyone told me I was crazy. I saw through her. She didn't break me. I made the choice to separate myself from her. As a result I miss out on seeing the rest of the family—my nieces, nephews and sister-in-law, at the holidays. My husband is very supportive of what I need to do for me."

Anila's Soul Writing

She needs to know there is someone to care for him and to mirror him in her death. My teacher sees me. I care for her and she appreciates my care. She's always caring for others. He needs to be reminded of unbridled emotion, less of control, of connection of his importance. He needs a mirror and when she's gone it will be me. I am enough. I am all I need. I must stop numbing my emotions and intuition with alcohol. I now have safe space to let it out. He

loves unconditionally. I am not too much. I am. Enough. I am all
I need. I have all the power within me.

It can seem like a curse or a blessing to be reunited with someone you once loved dearly in a past life. On the one hand, it brings back a wave of emotional bliss that is unlike anything you have experienced in this life. On the other, it also brings with it all of the issues you did not resolve from your previous incarnation together. For Anila, finding this great love again has been a little of both.

In this life, her former love is a body worker and she found him in her search for relief from her chronic condition. Being with him has triggered a considerable amount of bleed through for her to contend with in this life, including issues surrounding her physical karma. As an example, she said that during a bodywork session with him, he put pressure on the spot where the needle pierced through her back and into her liver in the 1675 lifetime.

"My thought during this body work meditation was, 'I died for you, to see you again,'" she recalled. "I realize we are one. We are connected as all are in this universe. I got flashes of images from our 1675 life playing out like a movie through the last half of my session. There was lots of dancing, singing, swimming, fishing, holding hands, and always entranced by the wind."

During an energy healing session, Anila learned that the needle was energetically still lodged inside her body. She could feel a searing heat as the energy worker removed it. She realized that when she had the bodywork session with him, it had activated that energetic weapon. "This caused my increasing side and liver pain, my extreme emotional longing, and resulted in me searching for a past-life regressionist!"

Anila indicated she also has had graphic dreams about the torture she endured in that life. "Very often I see visions of the necklace of my skin that the torturer made from cut outs under my left arm over my rib cage; three slices that he made into loops and wore as amulets on a necklace."

Unlike my other research subjects, Anila and I worked together on two different regressions (800 B.C. and 1675 A.D.) within two weeks of each other. I asked Anila how she felt each life was connected, not only to each other, but also to her—with special emphasis on how they are connected to her chronic condition.

"I believe that the start of my liver issues came from the anger of my torturer in 800 B.C.," she explained. "Physically he abused and tortured me, while energetically he unleashed rage and hate. Once he learned I had befriended his son it was even more so. I feel that in that last beating, which resulted in the loss of my life, that emotional energy was lodged in my liver as I was repeatedly hit and kicked on the right side of my ribcage and back. In the 1675 life, I also endured a blow to the right rib cage and back. The energetic crystal that was used to end my life in 1675 was left there, which I believe exacerbated the congestion of my liver and magnified the emotions lodged there. I died at age 22 in 1675, and when I turned 22 in this life I began having episodes of explosive anger, frustration, loneliness and isolation, and the feeling like I was looking for someone; a longing I could not explain. Until I met him again, I assumed it was related to my alcoholic and emotionally-absent father. I continued to add my own emotions, trapping them in the liver as I acted normal and okay, but had continued emotional turmoil. No one understood so I felt more isolated.

"When I met my current husband I was introduced to his mother. I now know her to be the reincarnation of my torturer from 800 B.C.. I just always knew she did not like me though I did nothing to provoke her or encourage ill will. Her anger, self-loathing, and dissatisfaction with her own life drove her to drinking. There was just this growing energetic divide between us. My husband was never very close to her, and I think she was jealous that he made something of himself and found someone to love him unconditionally. I felt wounded by her and started to distance myself as I realized there was nothing I could do to make her like me. I had to reserve my energy for my children and healthy relationships."

Anila's health issues began in 2006, a year after she met her mother-in-law. For many years after that, western medical doctors told her there was nothing wrong with her. She knew better.

"I believe my interaction with my mother-in-law's energy activated the emotional and physical karma in my liver, which also led to spleen deficiency and digestive issues that led to leaky gut and an immune disorder."

Anila was reunited with her former lover in 2009. "In that moment I looked into his eyes I thought, 'I must be with him,' which I brushed off as odd and socially unacceptable since I was seven months pregnant and married, and he had a family. I went to his classes and although I had a hard time being vulnerable with men I just always felt this openness and connection with him. I had some major energetic and emotional releases during some of his classes, and he always knew something had occurred. I kept myself at a distance from him except in class, feeling ashamed at how much I desired to be near him and be in his presence. Society doesn't teach you how to handle this."

She experienced a re-awakening within after she attended a group retreat that he was leading. During a bodywork session with him she said they both had an unexplainable energetic experience. That is when her liver issues became magnified.

"I believe this was because the energetic weapon still lodged in me was activated by the energy of all of our past lives together, melding into that one bodywork session. I started having physical pain in my right ribcage/torso and in the spot where the weapon was in addition to the pre-existing liver qi deficiency/stagnation."

In her body scan, Anila said her liver "ached" and then added that she had a spot in the upper farthest left corner of her stomach where she was experiencing pain. Thinking about where she was injured in both lifetimes, I asked Anila to discuss if the location of her past-life injuries was causing her any discomfort today—including whether there was a birthmark in those areas.

"I actually looked and found a smaller-sized mole directly over the top of the energetic weapon line in the upper leftmost part of my liver near the centerline of my body," she answered. "The physical pain in my rib cage and liver was basically gone except for the one spot that ran from front to back. Recently my energy healer removed the energetic weapon that was still there and now that is gone. I am still trying to heal the liver qi stagnation, which my practitioner says is stored anger and emotion."

Anila also indicated in the body scan that she has pain in her rib cage that "sometimes burns" and that she reported multiple moles and/or birthmarks in various parts of her body. I asked if she believed now if any of those were related to past-life injuries.

"All of the moles on my collarbone, back of neck, and the shoulder pain were related to the physical injuries I sustained from being racked during my torture and life in 800 B.C.," she said. "The mole on my big toe and my knee pain was also related to the 800 B.C. life when I was hobbled. The forehead mark I believe is from where I fell to the ground in 1675."

Anila stated in the initial project questionnaire that she has been dealing with feelings of overwhelming loneliness and despair since she was 22. Add to that she has had bouts of anger and suppressed emotions that she believes has contributed to the liver deficiency. I asked her to draw the parallel between what she was feeling in her previous lives with what she is feeling today and how they tie in to her physical condition.

"I believe some of the anger was lodged there by my torturer in 800 B.C. and I added to it during this life because I felt unseen, unheard, and alone," she said. "The despair I believe was activated at 22 because that is how I felt in 1675 when I was isolated and alone and waiting for my lover. I felt I desperately needed him and I felt incredibly lonely in 800 B.C. until my torturer's son befriended me. I also felt lonely in 1675 before I met my lover again and after he was gone. When my lover died in 1675 my last feelings were of despair and loneliness and I vowed to find him again. At age 22 in this life I believe these feelings were activated to a greater degree. At that point I became more and more aware I was different from others and I was searching for something or someone I just couldn't find. I added onto my stored emotions in my liver."

In the death scenes from two of her past lives, her misery was ended thanks to being aided by individuals who were related to their tormentors. I asked Anila what she saw as the connection between those individuals then and her relationship with them now.

"In both of the past lives my aides in death were the same soul as my meditation teacher in this life. She is helping me learn to let go of my suffering. Because of her age I am also getting a chance to take care of her in some ways and still provide her unconditional love as I did in 800 B.C. and wanted to do again."

Kaoolct's last thoughts were that he must always be strong; live from the heart when necessary; that sometimes with great sacrifice also comes great gifts. He hoped some day he would have the chance again to watch over that boy who is now Anila's meditation teacher. Anila's last thoughts from the 1675 lifetime were to find her lover again; wanting to not be lonely; willing to do anything; waiting as long as it takes. I asked how have those last thoughts manifested in subsequent or her current lifetime?

"I lived from my heart in 1675 and in my early years of this life I did so freely," she said. "I walled off my heart starting in my early teens and finishing that wall around age 22, so I am now having to chip away at that and open my heart again. I have the chance, due to my meditation teacher's age in this life, to do for her and care for her. I also am receiving the gifts of learning to surrender, opening my heart, and letting go of suffering. I found my lover again but only as a friend. I believe my sacrifice in this life is that I must forego a romantic relationship with him, but the gifts I receive are his friendship, a relationship with my teacher, my husband and children. I still am willing to wait to be with him romantically in another life, but I feel that is more likely to happen because I am learning the lessons I am supposed to learn before we are together again. I also believe he and my meditation teacher are learning theirs."

I asked Anila what the message in her soul writing—"I am enough. I am all I need"—meant to her in terms of her past lives and current condition.

"I got very comfortable suffering for love in my past lives," she admitted. "I also focused so much on the love I held for others that I neglected the love for myself. In this life letting go of my suffering, loving myself, and realizing I am really all I need and am enough to have joy are all part of my lessons."

Here we see a pattern that goes back nearly 3,000 years. Her soul has suffered much for love, unable to find a life where she had a peaceful existence. Yet she appears to be an advanced soul, having a guardian angel (guide) appear to help her transition, and serving as a role model to others about unconditional love. I asked Anila to elaborate on her insights into this and how it has impacted her current life.

"I have always been recognized as someone with a big heart and as a child I loved everyone," she said. "I began walling off my heart because I just could never grasp how mean people were to each other. As I've started un-walling my heart again, letting my love shine, and not caring if it receives a negative response, I am feeling much more myself and fulfilled. The realization of karma and divine justice, which does not play by the rules of human justice, has opened my eyes and heart again."

Many of the moles/marks she described in the scan are remnants of Kaoolct's life. I asked Anila if knowing their origin helped alleviate the discomfort associated with them.

"Within days of the session my shoulders, which had been aching more since my first regression, were pain free," she said. "Activities that used to aggravate them have not been. It's amazing!"

Those marks were predominantly the past-life scars given by her past-life torturer/present-life mother-in-law who, from what Anila said, still has not learned the lesson at hand. While there is still time for resolution and change may come, it may not happen until death and even then there is no guarantee. The presence of her mother-in-law in this life has provided lessons for both souls and an opportunity to transcend this karma.

"I believe I serve as a reminder to her of who she could be and how she could live her life," Anila said. "I ended my relationship with her in this life in 2014. I have since realized I need to show her forgiveness. That does not have to include a relationship but my forgiveness alone may be enough to soften her heart. By running from her in 1675, and running again in this life, it was an act of self-preservation but I was not noticing the karmic role it had for both of us. Now that I am aware, I also know how it could continue to affect me and what part my ego had in running from her this time. I think it was a big part of my lesson not to continue suffering by ending my relationship with her and not participating in that karmic spiral. I've been working on a letter to her. I feel like making some amends with her will help heal my liver stagnation."

Anila said that during the regression, her 800 B.C. life seemed more like a dream even though it felt so real. She speculated that it felt that way because it was harder for her to imagine a life going back that far.

"I could barely believe how I could feel the wind, and water, and smell the air in both lives," she explained. "Now when the wind blows I feel those sensations on a whole other dimension. I always feel like my lover from 1675 is holding my hand now when I feel the wind. Emotionally it was a little unnerving at how real it felt, but also a relief because it explained to me so much about how I had felt since age 22 and since meeting my lover and our teacher."

The combination regression/soul writing session had a positive impact on Anila and several months later she said she was still trying to process all she saw and learned.

"Not feeling 'crazy' anymore is a huge stepping stone for me," she said. "I have been able to put some words and reasons to feelings that I have had since the age of 22, and especially those around my teacher. Although I sometimes am feeling emotionally overwhelmed, lonely and confused, I am able to understand why it is so intense, so it is easier to process and let go. I also have been able to come to terms with having my teacher as a friend and am working on building a strong friendship. I think the most important impact is that it has helped me accept myself as I am and remember how I was before I bound myself into societal rules and norms."

As a result of our work together, Anila said her shoulder aches and tightness issues felt much better the day of the session and by the next day were gone. The ache in her right side/liver improved dramatically. When the energy worker removed the energetic weapon that was still lodged in the upper left part of her liver/abdomen, the rest of the discomfort and pain went away.

"You have given me a part of my life, heart, and soul back through these sessions," she said. "It was supposed to be my year of self-care and love and this has only helped that."

Death Before Dishonor

In the years I have been conducting past-life research, I have met several souls who claimed to be the reincarnation of some-one famous. There are numerous plausible reasons for their coming to that conclusion—so many, in fact, that an entire book can be written on this subject. I try to make no judgment when this occurs, even though the majority of them have little basis for their conclusion other than a resonance to a particular time period or historic character. Instead, I listen intently to their story to understand why they feel such a kinship to a particular personality. Thus their story becomes more significant than their identity.

My research projects have introduced me to many fascinating people, but I admit no one was quite like Jack. This 37-year old former Navy Corpsman with the Maine Corps and Operation Iraqi Freedom veteran walked in barefoot, wearing a Confederate Civil War cap and said he did so to honor the men in Confederate General Stonewall Jackson's army. I did not understand his affinity for Jackson until he revealed he believed himself to be not only the reincarnation of Jackson, but also of the Scottish Sir William Wallace (a/k/a Braveheart). Jack was keenly aware of his other lifetimes as well, but it was Jackson's life that was in the forefront. He explained why.

"Back in early 2009, my best friend from high school, who was a Civil War enthusiast, told me that I should begin to study General Jackson because he was interesting. I nagged him to tell me why because I soon saw the obvious similarities, to which he replied: 'Well, back in high school I noticed that you acted a lot like Jackson and I wondered why.'"

While his friend noticed behavioral similarities, he missed the most obvious—that in fact Jack is the spitting image of Jackson!

During his senior year in high school, Jack developed tendonitis in the base of both his middle fingers—first the left hand, then the right—which he said felt like a musket ball under his skin. "My dad shot muzzle loader rifles, so I knew what a ball looked and felt like," he explained. "Jackson was shot in the left hand, first at Manassas and almost lost the finger, and then at Chancellorsville a smooth bore musket ball lodged under the skin of his right hand. I also suffered tendonitis in both my left shoulder and elbow while on the high school golf team. Jackson was shot in both places at Chancellorsville, requiring amputation of the arm. I still have the remnant of a small birthmark on my left forearm matching the entry wound to Jackson's left forearm. During my first visit to Lexington, Virginia in 2009, I went to the Stonewall Jackson Memorial Cemetery and as I caught a first glimpse of Jackson's statue I felt an icy cold 'shot' through my left shoulder. I laughed at this because I knew what it meant. Then it occurred to me that Jackson had been shot by his own men at Chancellorsville and I had been shot at by my own men in Nasiriya, Iraq."

Hypnosis and dowsing opened Jack up to further psychic capacities and now he sometimes channels other aspects of his past lives, which manifest in seeing parallel historical timelines, gaining a strange talent, or craving. Sometimes his speech patterns subtly alternate between Irish/ Scottish and an antiquated Virginian/ Appalachian dialect, although no such dialect surfaced in our session.

Jack believes that the chronic conditions challenging him today are those he acquired from Jackson's life. According to Jack, they both had problems with equilibrium, eyesight, digestive disorders, and anxiety and that he still suffers with dyspepsia, acid reflux, and ulcers.

"Jackson believed if he bent over he would kink his intestines, which may be linked to Wallace having been disemboweled at his execution," Jack explained. "I've suffered sharp abdominal pains that don't last long and cannot be provoked.

Jackson believed one side of his body was longer than the other and felt the need to raise one arm in the air to drain the blood back to his core. I have a habitual need to crack my back to similarly balance myself. Wallace was tortured on the rack, and my joints have always cracked loudly since infanthood."

In terms of emotional issues, Jack said that Wallace had to keep his relationship with his wife, Marion, secret from the king and while pregnant with Wallace's child, Marion was arrested and executed. Jackson, a secretive man, married his first wife, Elinor, in a small, quiet ceremony and 14 months afterward, she died during childbirth.

"In 2006, I worked closely with an attractive female Corpsman named Carol at a Marine Corps Reserve center," Jack said. "I admit, my instincts told me to marry her but for once I disobeyed my instincts and kept things professional. After exactly 14 months at the command, Carol developed a very painful ovarian cyst and had to be put on light duty. Soon after, I left active duty and didn't see her again. A psychic reading told me that Marion, Elinor, and Carol were incarnations of the same spirit. I tend to fear relationships and am particularly petrified of marriage. Jackson always felt responsible yet helpless to the amount of death of women in his lifetime. I'm a good person but tend to sabotage, piss off, and emotionally hurt women to keep them from loving me. I desire women in my life, but isolate myself and avoid them due to my own emotional toxicity."

Unlike the majority of my project participants who were curious but unsure about the connection between their past life and their chronic condition, Jack was positive his current life condition stemmed from a previous life experience.

"Over the past six years, I've identified over 30 possible incarnations for myself," he said. "My undisciplined research has done very well to teach me about who I really am. We don't even have to talk about what I've divulged, but maybe let spirit tell its story. I am a good writer and counselor in my own right, but I have too much information and too little structuring to present it in a believable way. I need help and I can be of help, too. I'm willing to do as much or as little as you ask. This is part of my soul's purpose."

All of this, as fascinating as it was, paled by comparison to what came next. When I attempted to do the body scan, instead of identifying discomfort, sensitivity or birthmarks from this life, Jack immediately dictated a list of physical conditions from nearly all of his previous lifetimes.

He began by telling me he sensed nails in his feet and an arrow in his right thigh. When asked about his reproductive system, he said he had been castrated, mutilated and his guts were spilling out. A sword had cut into his kidneys. He had malaria and a spear went through his right upper quadrant. His intestines had been removed. His heart was stabbed from the back. He reported a scar on his left arm that he said was highlighted by a birthmark. His hands, like his feet, had been pierced and his fingers broken. His back had been broken and his tailbone had been fractured. Both shoulders had been dislocated or worse, one or both may have been removed. He experienced chronic choking and felt he had either been hanged or strangled to death. He had experienced brain trauma in the form of a concussion and felt burning in his eyes and ringing or deafness in his ears. His teeth had been removed and his jaw had been broken on his left side.

So Jack, other than that, how the heck are you?!?

I was curious which of those lifetimes we would explore, but he surprised me by going to a life in Judea in the year 38

A.D., which he proceeded to describe in extraordinary detail. He was a 42-year-old male named Huartah. He wore leather sandals and a long robe made of a brown flannel material with a few light-colored stripes going across toward the end of the robe. A maroon-colored belt was around his waist and tied at the left hip. He was 6' tall with an olive-colored complexion and blue eyes. His hands were well cared for and clean, as if he did not do any work. He wore two gold rings on the right hand. His light reddish brown hair had a slight wave to it. He had a beard and wore nothing on his head.

Huartah had been orphaned at a young age and taken as a ward of the royal family. He was a strong boy who picked up skills quickly and although he started out as a servant, his demeanor led him to be groomed into a soldier. Huartah lived in the city center comprised of mud and brick houses that he described as "very Mediterranean looking." He was on the third floor of a building that stood on a hill overlooking homes and markets. The landscape was mountainous and the ocean was nearby.

His evening meal was taken at a friend's house where they were seated at a heavy hardwood table. They dined on mutton, olive salad, and flatbread. He did not use utensils, although he reported seeing a knife on the table. He ate out of a fire-kiln dish and wooden bowls. "We're both rather wealthy," he said. He and his friend were "discussing business of some gravity."

When asked what his feelings were toward his friend, he said, "We were in the military together. We've known each other a long time. Now we work for the government and advise on government security. Things are turning sour and we're deciding on our loyalties and whether we can continue doing our job, turn whistle blowers, or lead a rebellion. He has

130

less of a problem with the government than I do and I knew he couldn't see what I saw."

At what would be their last meal together, Jack said they were discussing options. "I felt compelled to decide if he was really my friend or not before taking any action. I was hoping he'd see what was going on and convince me I wasn't crazy or not alone and he'd pledge his support to join me. I was probably asking too much and this move was very risky. I felt pretty confident that he was turning toward my side. He listened patiently, disciplining his reactions to my words. He attempted to ease my anxieties, but beneath the feigned serenity, he was terrified at the news I shared with him. It wouldn't be a surprise if he didn't want to believe me since he often found my hyper vigilance irritating, but he appreciated it as well. He didn't think the way I did and thus failed to anticipate the pending treachery. My paranoia may have been justified, but now I had doubts about my friend as well. Did he believe me? Was he working against me? Would he help me do something about the corruption or at least escape with me?"

The friend hesitated to act and once he did, it was too late. "Events moved so quickly, neither he nor I would have had time to do anything," he said. "If I could, I would have taken the first boat out to sea."

What happened next became the significant traumatic event in Huartah's life. While walking down a quiet street he was ambushed and attacked by an unknown group of assailants, armed with clubs. "I guarded with my left arm and attacked with my right," he explained. "My left arm was struck and broken and my right knee was struck from the side, causing me to fall. I curled up to protect myself but they kept kicking me in the back," he said. "I think they were trying to kill me. I kept getting up to fight back but there were too many of them. I was telling myself 'I am a strong man. I fought wars but I can't get them away from me.' I felt I might be injured internally. I couldn't fight any more. I felt weak and faint. They finally left."

Huartah called the attack calculated, adding, "If it were a random mugging I could fight them off and they would have quit sooner. I never saw them before and their faces were covered. I thought: 'What if my friend turned me in?' He was the only person I spoke to since our conversation five or six hours earlier. Maybe he wasn't honest with me or I misread him. I jumped to conclusions like 'he sold his soul' and 'maybe the wealth and power went to his head.' He liked his position and it was all he ever wanted. I joined the military to defend Rome and that's when we met. After the campaign finished, our successes led to a security job opportunity with the government. It wasn't what I wanted to do but he talked me into it. Once inside, I learned how government corruption worked. I wanted to fight it, get away from it, or expose it. He didn't see the need for things to change."

When asked why Huartah was such a threat to the government, Jack said, "I was very observant, secretive, and resourceful. If anyone could bring down the house of cards, I could. I had too much access. I got in too deep."

Huartah survived the attack, but became very sick, with pain in his right kidney. "I stumbled home. Nobody was around. I tried to tell people what happened, but no one wanted to listen to me. I couldn't get a doctor. The only people in my life were those I worked with, but they were told to avoid me. The peasants I sometimes befriended weren't around. No one would talk to me. I was pretty desperate. I knew I was dying.

This was bad. I just laid down and prayed I would get better, but I never did."

In desperation, Huartah found himself in front of the home of a pretty, 20-something widow. Even though they were strangers, she recognized him because he was somewhat famous in the area. She cared for him and he realized they had met before. He wanted to stay with her but the fantasy of a relationship with this woman was ended when authorities came to arrest him for treason. He was taken away and quickly sentenced to the common form of execution: death by crucifixion. His eyelids were cut off and he was nailed through the hands and feet to two planks, fixed in the shape of an X. Huartah was horrified to see his friend had been similarly crucified, but felt relieved that maybe he had not been betrayed after all. Within the same day, the two friends died together.

At the moment of death, Huartah said he had mixed feelings. "I could trust nobody," he said. "I didn't regret my service but I questioned whether it was worth dedicating my life and ending up that way or whether I should have had a family. I thought of the woman who rescued me and I wondered, 'Why did I not marry her and have a family?' My last thoughts were of my friend and the kind widow woman and I decided that was enough family for this lifetime."

In terms of any unfinished business, he said, "Leaving the military and taking that job in the government compromised my values to be there. I didn't trust myself enough. I looked outside of myself for others to show approval. I never had that. I seemed very brave, decisive and had leadership but that triggered feelings of insecurity and insufficiency."

When exploring similarities between his past and his current lives, Jack said the pain in his kidneys persists in this life.

No matter how much he tries to treat it, it doesn't go away. "I thought it was adrenalin fatigue," he said. "I feel regret and remorse. Digestion—that worry, constant anxiety—what have I gotten myself into? What's going to happen to me?"

In terms of anyone from that life in his life now, Jack said he thought the woman who took care of him seemed familiar to him in this life but he thought she was a former girlfriend he dated while stationed in Bahrain. The friend is a man he worked with in the Navy. "In this life we were such good friends. I ended up in Baltimore and he in Arlington and we left the Navy. He disappeared. This guy wasn't a bad guy. We couldn't have intimacy in this life. We were very similar in that life. He was incredibly loyal to his boss and officers. Superficial work relationships."

Jack gave additional insights about Huartah, remembering that his father had been a merchant and his mother a craftswoman. His parents abandoned him when he was around 12 years old. "His loyalty was a reflection of that," Jack said. "He wanted something to serve. Huartah never trusted anyone after being abandoned, although he was considered an adult by that age, which led to his hyper vigilance and subsequent success as a military leader. It also prepared him to see the warning signs of his demise."

Considering that this life took place in Judea a few years after Jesus' death, I asked Jack if he thought Huartah might have crossed paths with Jesus. "He had access to the government's knowledge of Him," he answered. "Kind of like Edward Snowden. That might have been a factor here. Meeting someone like Jesus and knowing the government structure— wrestling with his authentic self vs. governmental role. Closest I could think of was the story of the Roman Centurion in the book of Matthew 8: 5-13, who said his servant was suffering with palsy, and asked Jesus, 'Could you help?' He was definitely a man of faith. I wonder if he was at the crucifixion. Was he so deeply engrained with Jesus that he felt sympathetic pain?"

Jack's Soul Writing

Caesar has his job. You have yours.
Never doubt again. Go in trust.
Death before dishonor.
We are the actors
I lost my fight, my strength left me.
Honor is uncomfortable.
Can I ever trust again? Who am I? What does this mean?
I have made a grave mistake.
What have I done? What should I do?
This is far bigger than I am.
If there's God where is it now?
Missed opportunities and fraudulent life.
What's the use—I'm tired—I want to fight but I can't.
This lifetime feels like a big mistake.
Why doesn't anyone else see the obvious?
I can never look the other way on unlawfulness.
Family is trouble. I hide—I fight—I hide again.
Not enough time.

After our session, Jack had no dreams or spontaneous memories of that lifetime but the way he felt the rest of that week seemed significant. "I was depressed and the vision played out in the back of my mind," he explained. "The feelings of betrayal and failure were strong. My physical condition didn't change at all. The insomnia, ulcer, choking and adrenal fatigue are still present. This is probably due to having so many layers of traumatic lifetimes since Lemuria/Atlantis."

As he returned to ponder my follow-up questions, he said he was changing and resolving some of these issues as he gained more understanding. "The issues with my parents don't seem so bad anymore and I have less fear over my survival because I saw what I faced in that past lifetime. It felt real and my definition of authority has changed. It's brought me closer to center."

Jack talked about Huartah being ambushed, being kicked in the back and having internal bleeding. I asked if any of those injuries coincided with any physical condition he might be dealing with in this life.

"Jackson had, and I have, dyspepsia, duodenal ulcers and adrenal dysfunction," he said. "I had colic as a baby and many complications from digestion in my teen years. I'm fairly certain that during his time in the Roman legion, Huartah was wounded in the upper abdomen during a battle in his 20s. This wound plagued him for the rest of his life. I don't have any birthmarks or scars to back this up. However, my ulcer began around age 25 and the kidney started around age 33. I'm now 37. Jackson had related issues at these same ages with no known cause, but Dr. Hunter Holmes McGuire, who was chief surgeon of Jackson's Corps, noted that once the battle began, those symptoms seemed to resolve themselves. There is a definite part of me that likes battle as well and this seems to make my problems subside."

Huartah talked about having a meal at his friend's home where he discussed a situation he wanted to change. At first he believed the ambush was the result of his friend's betrayal. In Jack's initial questionnaire, he said he had digestive problems. I asked if he saw any correlation between those problems and the betrayal happening at a meal.

"That person was my closest friend I've ever had in this current life and other lifetimes as well," he said. "He was a veteran of the war in Afghanistan before I met him, so you could say he's very much the Dr. Watson to my Sherlock Holmes. This guy was a comrade in arms in this lifetime and during the Civil War. He would have sacrificed himself for me. Without a stable family life, Huartah grew up to be hyper vigilant, which in this setting overflowed into paranoia. His friend was trying to calm him down, listen, and sincerely help whichever way he could. Huartah mistook his friend's congenial, cavalier attitude as apathy, but he actually was projecting a strong front. Both men were frightened, but the friend hadn't been as aware of what was taking place until Huartah told him.

"The threat to these two men and many others was that they had become sympathetic to the social movement started by Jesus of Nazareth," Jack continued. "Once Jesus had been executed, the Roman government targeted many of His followers for elimination. Huartah and possibly his friend were secretly following Jesus, first as spies but then as believers. They were suddenly forced to decide upon the direction of their loyalties. Siding with the Nazarene movement would be treason. Staying loyal to the government would mean that these men would be sent to hunt down innocent people. Huartah had come to know Jesus quite well by spying on Him and may have had personal interaction with Him as well. The only family Huartah had known was his adopted royal family and his fellow soldiers. How could he abandon what little family he had to protect the people following this Jesus of Nazareth? What did he owe any of them? After being cared for by the young widow, who turned out to be a follower of Jesus, Huartah understood the greater context of the situation."

During his body scan, Jack described sensitivities and discomforts in various parts of his body, the majority of which came from other lifetimes. I wondered, in looking at each one individually, if he saw any tie-in specifically with Huartah's life experience that would explain those sensitivities and discomforts.

> *Nails to his feet:* "I think Huartah may have survived the beating, thanks to the love shown to him by the widow," Jack said. "The authorities found him, charged him with treason, and after a show trial he, too, was crucified, with use of nails rather than rope."

> *Kidneys:* Over activity of the adrenal glands became the cause of his pain and anxiety of today. "As a soldier, Huartah would be trained to protect his stronger right arm in the attack, sacrificing his weaker left arm to block upper body attacks," Jack explained. "Doing so left him with a broken wrist. He then was guarding his left while defending with his right, exposing his right flank to attack. There was a kick to the right knee, which knocked him to the ground, face first. The attackers then stomped on his right side, injuring his right kidney. My pain is a nagging soreness, sometimes coldness, coupled with fatigue, so I think they were using clubs and feet. He still survived until he was executed a few days later."

Spear through right upper quadrant: "I had to meditate and dowse this one for deeper information," Jack said. "Turns out that during one of the battles Huartah fought while in the Roman legion, he was stabbed by a spear but recovered. He was around 25 years old. This wound probably plagued him the rest of his life."

Pierced hands; fingers broken: "After the attack, Huartah was found and arrested," Jack said. "He was then crucified with nails to the hands and feet. (The broken fingers were Jackson's being shot at 1st Manassas, May 1861 [left hand] and then Chancellorsville, May 1863 [right hand].) These wounds could even have been a type of karmic stigmata from Huartah's life."

Concussion: "Yes, Huartah was beaten almost senseless."

Burning eyes: "Sort of, because his eyelids were removed before his execution and the last sensations he felt before dying was the sun blazing into his eyes," Jack recalled. "Jackson experienced burning eyes frequently and would sometimes lose part of his vision to the point of significant disability. My experiences with these symptoms were not nearly as frequent or intense. My eyes often weep for no medical reason."

Huartah spoke of not trusting himself enough, of looking outside of himself to others to show approval and that while he had leadership skills and seemed very brave and decisive, that only triggered feelings of insecurity and insufficiency. I asked Jack if those feelings resonated to him in this life.

"As a child, I had many nightmares about being helpless and having inconsolable grief and remorse over failures and mistakes I made, not doing my soul's job but not fitting in with humanity either," Jack said. "In Huartah's life, he was orphaned and a ward of the royal family. In my life, I kept my parents this time but they are emotionally needy and manipulative. I was strong enough to break away from them but it was very traumatic for me to do so. It cost me nearly my whole family, not to mention my sanity. That's why I feel like I cannot make close relationships. I can endure the isolation of leadership but cannot open myself to intimate relationships."

By his admission, Jack still doesn't trust anyone. "I've never been married and whatever friends I once had didn't last," he said. "Any friend can betray you. Therefore any enemy can befriend you. My greatest fear right now is that I may likely die again before learning how to trust. I've tried different modalities: EFT, ho' ono pono, visualization, eye movement, etc. I'm still too close to the betrayal."

Jack is rebuilding his trust by opening himself to meeting new people in connection to things that are important to him. "As I volunteer at the Stonewall Jackson House in Lexington and am writing my bachelor thesis paper on him, I'm drawing more parallels between us," he said. "One of the other volunteers happens to be a William Wallace historian. UVA has their Department of Perceptual Studies (DOPS), which studies past-life memories in children. Having met one of their researchers, I may have something to offer them after graduation. So there is fodder for building professional relationships and a safe environment for learning to trust again."

We discussed the possibility of Huartah crossing paths with Jesus Christ, since he lived in Judea a few years after Jesus' death. In my soul writing, the message came that the connection to Jesus was deeper than what was revealed—and was the backstory that led to Huartah's conversion from government follower to one of conscience and authenticity. I asked Jack if he got any additional insights into that possibility.

"I can't tell how Huartah interacted with Jesus, except perhaps as the Roman Centurion whose servant suffered from palsy," he said. "This story resonates with me because of the soldier's genuine reverence and humility in the presence of Jesus."

Jack's soul incarnated in multiple lifetimes in which he served in the military. I asked why he chose to repeat military life experiences. What had it taught him? What were the common threads that ran through each life that connected to his physical issues?

"I was strongly attracted to the military and the military made me strong," he explained. "I've been just as involved with priesthoods as with military work. Religion has usually played a major role in my life, although I don't regularly attend church. I pray regularly and listen to my instincts. I also dowse and muscle test many of my life decisions. One place I'm greatly devoid is with children. Lifetime after lifetime, I'm either celibate or my children and wives keep dying on me. Even Jackson only met his daughter, Julia, for the first time a month before he died. Dang me. Well, one exception was a pre-Christian lifetime where I had umpteen wives and a bazillion children, but I think I've been banned from doing that again."

In his soul writing, Jack wrote: "This lifetime feels like a big mistake. Why doesn't anyone see the obvious? I can never look the other way on unlawfulness." I asked Jack if he still felt that way.

"I'm a pathological crusader and also have a long memory," he said. "It's easy for me to see recurrences of the same patterns in history. From economic exploitation to sexual depravity, it's all been done before and I'm keenly aware of it. I wish I had a more effective way to share this with people but they don't want to hear any of it."

Another interesting notation in his soul writing was: "Family is trouble. I hide—I fight—I hide again." I asked if he saw that pattern repeating in his present life.

"I seem to be the type of person who others easily forget," he said. "I step in or speak up periodically when something needs to be done but I'm not a constantly present force. Even my current lifetime suggests this, which is what is meant by 'I hide-I fight-I hide again.' During OIF (Operation Iraqi Freedom) I was pictured on the cover of *Newsweek*, which caused a small firestorm back home, but after my return from deployment, there was a deafening silence and lack of a homecoming. This perplexes me, except that I suppose it's actually the way I wish it to be. It hurts not to be involved in celebrations, especially my own, but it's what makes me effective. My heroism is my best-kept secret."

The theme of seeing things for what they truly were, wanting to change them, exposing them and then paying the ultimate price, has occurred repeatedly in Jack's previous lifetimes. The issues of abandonment and betrayal were cast against his authenticity, honesty and desire to do good works and change society. His soul's mission appeared to be about to see through what presents itself as truth, expose its dark side and effect change. I asked Jack if he felt that was true.

"My memory is long and I don't take kindly to being fooled or betrayed but I take my rage out on myself," he explained. "Just like when Jesus said, 'forgive them for they know not what they do,' I understand that those around me are fast asleep, ignorant, etc. It pisses me off because they're all too happy to stay asleep. I've had childhood nightmares of my voice dropping to a whisper although I'm trying to scream. I still get this feeling when I get sleep paralysis. I try to scream but can barely clear my throat. This is related to my self-image in relation to the world around me."

As aware of his past lives as he was, Jack said he did not know about Huartah. That is what made his findings all the more intriguing. Having worked with his other past lives so intently for so long, I asked him to describe what the regression segment was like for him in terms of clarity of images, emotions, and understanding and how did his senses respond on all levels.

"My visions are never as vivid as my dreams and I still have doubts about what I'm experiencing," he said. "Since learning techniques from Robert Monroe lectures and Burt Goldman's lessons, I'm far more flexible and creative to quantum jump in and out of places. My challenge is getting deep enough in trance to make the experience real. I am usually removed from the events occurring, being aware from a first person perspective, but I carry the understanding that I'm no longer there. I need to focus on smell and taste to gain information from those senses. Visual is my first input, then emotional, then tactile. Auditory is strong but also requires more focus to gain information. My mind is often distracted with other processing thoughts and experiences, especially when my mind is relating things like other past life or childhood experiences."

Jack acknowledged that our session impacted his life, although for the most part his condition remained the same. For him, the regression revealed a lifetime that was very closely patterned with his current lifetime and that of Jackson's.

"My ulcer is improving but still stings and though my adrenals are not completely burnt out they definitely smart like a stubbed toe sometimes," he said. "Just when I start getting an upper hand on this ailment, insomnia definitely relapses me every time. My insomnia and anxiety are significant. I cannot digest food properly. I've only recently stopped drinking but I now self-medicate with lots of herbal supplements."

For Jack, the regression revealed a lifetime that was very closely patterned with his current life and that of Jackson's. "As I better understand Jackson's 'hypochondria' as bleed through past-life memories, I understand my own related health issues," he said. "Also, it expands on my relationship to Jesus, which again explains the shared religious traits between His and my lifetimes. I'm less likely to fear my separation from my parents and lack of close friends. It's consistent with my soul identity. Also, I am adjusting my eating to a semi-vegetarian, minimalist diet like that of Jackson and Huartah. I always knew I couldn't eat my family's mass quantities of meat and potatoes diet. I feel more permission to be who I am—fair but not necessarily nice—even if it means kicking the shit out of someone about to kick the shit out of me. It's taken this long to accept that it's okay for me to fight, argue, and not have to be friends with everyone."

Chapter Six

Drugs & Alcohol

"Drink today, and drown all sorrow;
You shall perhaps not do it tomorrow."
— John Fletcher, *The Bloody Brother*

Understanding the source of an addictive behavior can do much to hasten the healing process. In "Karma as Memory," published in the April-June 2013 issue of *Venture Inward*, Kevin J. Todeschi and Henry Reed wrote:

"Negative karmic memory can include such things as unresolved anger, biases, animosities, addictions, and other unresolved attachments that prevent the soul from experiencing wholeness within itself. These memories must be faced and resolved, essentially creating a change in consciousness or an expanded personal awareness. For example, the memory of addictive patterns must be reawakened with the very first cigarette or the very first glass of beer. How the individual deals with that reawakened memory in the present will determine a portion of his or her life experience."

Initially I had decided not to work with individuals who were dealing with drug or alcohol addictions, but because both Meg and Christopher came to me by what I felt was divine intervention, I knew I had to include their stories.

By the time they came to the project, they both were recovering alcoholics and had been sober for a considerable amount of time, so the purpose of including them in the project was more about how events in their past lives triggered their addictive behavior in this life.

Mary Ann Woodward discussed the issue of alcohol from a karmic perspective. "Today alcoholism is recognized as a disease. It frequently seems to be a karmic condition, which can be traced to overindulgence in one or more prior lives. . . . Several individuals who apparently entered this earth-experience with a proclivity towards alcoholism, based on earlier excesses that may have contributed to their downfall in the past, were warned to avoid overindulgence and beware of strong drink or alcohol in any form."

This would be the case for Meg, a 62-year-old retired travel professional. Meg's soul group in this life included her fellow workers—the same souls who had been part of her inner circle in an 18th century life where drinking and doing drugs was their primary pasttime. Once these souls connected in a social environment in this life, the old pattern of drinking resurfaced and Meg, who did not drink prior to reconnecting with this group, soon succumbed to her past-life aspect's behavior.

For Christopher, it was all about the issue of self-worth, of free will, and of choosing a behavior and a path that would lead to his ultimate freedom. Like most souls, he experienced the constant struggle between good and evil; love and hate; comfort and pain. The story of why the dark side was prevalent for so long in this life and how he managed to move through it is a classic story of karmic redemption.

According to Edgar Cayce there is no general outline of treatment for alcoholic cases—or really, any chronic conditions. This was clearly stated in reading 606-1.

> (Q) In alcoholic cases, can a general outline of treatment be given?
> (A) No. Each individual has its own individual problems. Not ALL are PHYSICAL...

Serving Others to Stay Sober

Meg had been a member of the A.R.E. for many years and had been regressed before. We met for brunch when we were both in Virginia Beach and after I told her about my upcoming research project, she asked if I considered alcoholism an eligible chronic condition. "I am a recovering alcoholic," she admitted. "I feel my addiction has a direct connection to a past life, which I have chosen to fix in this life by embarking on a program of sobriety. Every day I make a conscious choice not to pick up a drink." After she told me her story, there was no doubt in my mind that she'd be an excellent subject for my research.

Meg regressed to the year 1712 where she lived in a town in the Provence region of France. Her name then was Lawrence Orlean, a 30-year-old man with "pinky white" skin. He wore white stockings over his knees and had on low-heeled shoes with buckles—"the shoes of a dandy," Meg laughed. He wore yellow silk pants, a long-sleeve shirt with lace cuffs, covered by a vest and a jacket. His white wig was tied in a ponytail. His real hair was brown and straight, not long enough to be in a ponytail, and he held a hat in his hand.

Lawrence was in a town with narrow cobblestone streets and shops. The buildings were made of square stones and were several stories tall, with open windows. Shops were on the main floor with apartments above.

Lawrence took his evening meal of roast meat, potatoes and gravy in a public house. He ate off china, used silverware and drank ale out of a pewter mug. He said the bar maids were attracted to him because he was good looking and wealthy. He was joined by what he called his, "so-called friends, drinking, eating. I have money. That's probably why they like me. They are my drinking crowd. We hang out. It's what I know to be fun. I don't have to work—my family has money." He used the word "useless" but it wasn't clear if he felt his companions were useless or if he was talking about himself. He did say his companions were fun to be around but he had no deep connection to them. "I'm a shallow person and so are they," he admitted.

Lawrence's significant event was not so much an event as it was an attitude to life. He described himself as, "Very selfish. Only cared about myself and my pleasure. I didn't have to work so I did selfish, frivolous things. I hurt women. I didn't care. Became addicted. Lived only for myself. No purpose or service—only my own pleasure. I had those people as friends because I was no better a friend—only selfish. Maybe that's why I have to be unselfish in this life. To be sober you have to serve others. I didn't serve anybody because I didn't care about anybody. Now I have to stay sober to help others. What a useless fop."

When asked what his life was like, he said—"Day in and day out—lack of purpose. Pleasure seeker. Hanging out with other useless people."

His father was a well-to-do-merchant who accumulated enough money so he had status but not royalty. "I was spoiled—an only child—I got everything and then some, so I thought everyone should give me something," he said. "I think even though my parents were to blame for making my life so easy, I hurt them. They pampered me and then they didn't like the way I turned out. My father worked hard and produced this worthless son—even though they put me on the path by spoiling me."

Besides drinking, Lawrence abused opium. "I was uncaring and self-absorbed so I'm sure I hurt many along the way because I didn't care."

Lawrence died in what he called a "drug den" where everyone was sitting around stoned. He was 32 at the time of his death, caused by an overdose. "The room is very smoky so maybe I inhaled too much opium. I had been there for several days. I finally took too much."

His last thoughts were, "My life was worthless so I didn't mind leaving. My path was set. I couldn't go back. I had no skills. I thought this life was worthless. I knew better on another level that life has to have purpose and service and in that life I had none of that. I couldn't change. I gave up. Maybe the overdose was on purpose on another level. I didn't mind dying because I wasn't happy."

When asked about the similarity of Lawrence's life to her current life, Meg said, "As a child I was very smart and got all A's, but I was very domineering and controlling. Kids were afraid of me. I had to skip a grade. Nobody liked me because I was so obnoxious. I knew it was teaching me something. I couldn't get friends by being dominating and controlling. I had to learn to care about people. I wanted them to genuinely like me. My time in elementary school I carried Lawrence's arrogance until I skipped that grade."

Meg said her parents in this life didn't drink and that she didn't drink in high school or college. "I had an aversion to it and didn't respect people who drank at football games. I became addicted as a flight attendant."

Meg's Soul Writing

Lawrence knew his life was a waste. He knew on another level that he was wasting his "time"—opportunity but he felt it was too late to change. He was "corrupted" by his parents in the sense they spoiled him. He was their only son and they gave him everything, thinking it would make him happy and he would love them more. But it was just the opposite. The more they gave him the more contempt he had for them even though he knew they meant well. He also knew money had "ruined" his life by spoiling him. His soul "knew" that his life was a waste. But by then it was too late to change. He was physically incapable. In this life I had to learn how to care for others. On a deep level, I carried over my addiction to alcohol so I could learn that lesson. Alcoholics must serve others to stay sober.

Meg did not report any bleed through from our session. In revisiting her initial questionnaire, I reminded her that she was certain her present addiction to alcohol was past-life related. Considering what we saw of Lawrence's life, I asked if she felt it came from that lifetime or another that we did not explore.

"I feel very strongly that that life was the main experience dealing with the addiction to alcohol," she said. "I may have had tendencies in earlier lives preceding that one, but in that one it was out of control."

Lawrence referred to his "so-called friends" and said they probably only liked him because of his money. I asked whether those feelings resonated with her in this life and if so, how were they manifesting in terms of her challenges with alcoholism.

"I do not feel that I am just liked for my money," she said. "First of all, I'm not a rich, free spender. Secondly, I have always known—even at a young age—that I needed to develop myself from within so that I would be loved. I always felt that if I could cultivate a consciousness of love within myself, I would be loved for myself. Maybe that is the lesson I learned from that experience of being loved for my money rather than myself."

Lawrence called himself a "shallow person" and said he was "very selfish, only cared about myself and my pleasure." I asked Meg if that description fit how she felt about herself in this life—in other words, is that a carry over?

"When I was in elementary school I was extremely bright," she explained. "In 4th grade I was head of our class, team captain, etc., but felt I really intimidated kids into giving me those positions. Then my school (my teacher, etc.) decided to have me skip a grade. I went from top to the bottom. No one, except a few girls from my scout troop, knew me, and the new kids couldn't stand me. I was a big mouth, arrogant, know-it-all. It was so painful but I knew, even at 10 years old, that I had to change myself or no one would ever like me. That was really the beginning of my inner transformation from arrogant obnoxious brat to a better, kinder person. I feel I carried into this life those traits from my former life with the intention of overcoming them."

On the flip side, Meg indicated, "to be sober you have to serve others." I asked if she felt that was the lesson she was working on, and wondered if her choices have enabled her to be in a position of serving others to make up for that karma. She said that was absolutely true.

"My career has been serving others in a glorified waitress job," she said. "That job was fascinating and interesting and it took me all over the world. If I had had to serve others in a lesser position where I was miserable, I might have regressed, become bored and bitter, and not learned what I came here to learn. They say God never gives you more than you can handle. Although required to serve others, keep my opinions to myself, I was happy in my work environment. I think that made it easier to do and easier to grow."

Lawrence had some harsh criticisms of his parents, saying they spoiled him and gave him everything and then some, thus giving him the attitude that "everyone should give me something." He blamed his parents for making his life so easy and said he hurt them in return. I asked Meg if any of that resonated to the relationship she had with her parents in this lifetime and she said not at all.

"I have had two of the finest souls as parents in this life, but nothing was handed to me on a silver platter. I was expected to work for what I received, including my allowance as a child. There were always chores to be done. And if I needed extra money, I had to do more. When I wanted to take guitar lessons and we had no guitar, I had to earn half the money for it— which I did by selling boxes of greeting/birthday cards door to door. I was seven years old. I wanted to play so badly, I did it."

We know that no life is worthless, although Lawrence certainly considered his life as meaningless. Reflecting on that life, I asked Meg what she could say to Lawrence about some aspect of that life that did have meaning.

"I guess I could say I was generous in some respects. I spent money freely on my so-called friends. But since I didn't earn the money, I didn't really value it. I guess I knew there was always more where it came from."

Meg indicated in this life she was a very domineering and controlling child, carrying Lawrence's arrogance into this life. I asked what that taught her and how did she overcome that karma?

"By skipping a grade in elementary school, I think the wheels were set in motion for my lessons in learning humility to start," she explained. "It was so painful to suddenly be so disliked by kids who had not known me before that I could only think about what I could do to not hurt so much. At ten years old, that kind of rejection is almost unbearable, but it set me on the path of developing a kinder, gentler me."

Meg said that Lawrence felt that money had ruined his life by spoiling him. I asked about her attitude toward money today and how has that played out karmically.

"I was selfish when I was younger," she said. "I always saved my money because there was always something I wanted to do—like travel. But I have never cared about material displays like fancy cars, expensive clothes, etc. As I developed and became more conscious of the suffering in the world (my first job out of college was teaching music in Nairobi, Kenya) I realized my many blessings and have made a conscious effort to give my time and money to many causes. I believe now 'as ye sow so shall ye reap' and I have received plenty in return."

I had a sense that Meg's alcoholism was triggered by her fellow workers—that they were the same soul group who had been with her as Lawrence. I asked if she thought that was true and if so, what have they taught her.

"They may have been put in my path to start the ball rolling, i.e. my drinking," she said. "After the initial intro to alcohol, I pretty much drank on my own."

Meg said she was amazed at how clear the regression was and when I asked her to look for a year on the door, 1712 appeared clearly. "I knew this was the time/date I saw the inside of an inn with food, fire, smoky, tables, etc., very lively. I even knew I was wearing yellow silk pants and thought myself quite a dandy."

I asked Meg if our session impacted her life in any way and she said it had. "It helped to clarify why I have felt so strongly about certain inner aspects of my life and development. One of my gifts is a beautiful voice. When I was much younger I could have pursued a career using my voice. But there was always an inner 'voice' which said I could only use my voice for service. That to do otherwise would serve the ego and I would regress rather than progress in my life purpose and spiritual development."

Since Meg had her drinking under control prior to our session, the question regarding whether the session improved her condition did not matter in this instance. Instead I asked if she had any final thoughts.

"When you go to AA meetings, you realize the extent of this disease and the numbers worldwide who suffer from it," she said. "My only hope by sharing my own experiences is that someone who has the same disease and is still suffering will have an explanation for it and seek the help, which is readily available. I believe there are no accidents in life. There is always a reason they are suffering. The good news is, you don't have to keep on suffering and you don't have to suffer alone."

Embrace Your Power

Christopher, 44, came to me as the result of a referral by a psychologist colleague of mine who had been working with him for a while. As a result, by the time I saw Chris, he already was well into the healing process and that 20 years of injuries finally were being resolved. When we met in September of 2014, his greatest challenge was the recent loss of a job he described as "very toxic, but it did pay my bills."

During our body scan, Chris noted throbbing in his left foot and said his feet had been broken and put in braces. He reported an ankle injury and overall much foot trauma.

He had knee pain for years and talked about a hip injury. There was some sensation on the root chakra. He described discomfort in his left arm and upper back between his shoulder blades. There also was some discomfort in his right shoulder and sharp pain in his left shoulder. The right side of his neck held some discomfort and there was tingling on the left rear of his head. He described energy coming out of his third eye area.

Chris regressed to 234 A.D., somewhere in the Middle East. He saw himself as a tall, slender, dark Egyptian-like female in her 20s. Her feet were bare and she wore a "long, flowing, silky white dress" that was below her knees. She had black, lustrous silky hair adorned with a jeweled tiara. Her name began with a "B" but all Chris could ascertain was it sounded like "Bar" and the rest of it rhymed and flowed. For identification purposes, we will refer to her merely as Bar.

Bar was in her room in a "pretty, stone, white" building that overlooked a city that stretched below her. The building had flowing draperies and she described it as comfortable. She liked being in her room. From the building's vantage point, she could see the ocean.

She took her evening meal at a long table in the dinner hall, eating fruit, lamb, cheese, and drinking wine. There was a "rough looking man with black hair and beard, sitting at the table." There were several place settings on the table, but at that moment only the two of them were seated. "Seems like we're waiting for others," she says, speculating those others were family members. Servants brought food to the table. Later she said the man, "feels like my father" and that she has "more fear than love" toward him. "My father is worried and concerned, but I don't know why."

The significant event in this life was the death of Bar's mother and brother from an unknown sickness. She was a teenager at the time. Her 5-year-old brother was her only sibling. There was a sickness going through the city. Upon revealing this, Chris reported feeling a pain in his right knee. "Feel like that's my father's pain; the worry and hurt are around the sickness and the loss." Both her mother and brother died at the same time. She and her father did not contract the disease. "There's no love between father and me," she says. "Pain, hurt. No relationship."

When asked why there were settings at the table for her mother and brother long after they had died, she said that was per her father's instructions.

Bar further described her father as, "Viking-ish. Very hearty. Very barbaric. He provided comfort for family. He looks mean. He looks like somebody I wouldn't want to hang out with."

Even as an adult she never left their family home. "I don't feel like I ever leave. I feel isolated. He doesn't want me to leave. Fear of losing me."

When asked how she spent her day, she replied, "It doesn't feel like I do much of anything. I become friendly with the caretaker.

She's older. She's kind and she takes care of me. Grandmotherly. She was there when my brother and mother were alive."

Her father never remarries. "Seems like he holds me responsible [for their deaths]," Bar says. "I should have done something I didn't do. I should have known better—that it would get out of hand. It feels like a wisdom or knowledge that I didn't trust. I should have known it was coming before it came. I get warnings from places—I know things but I don't trust. I don't think they're real. I don't listen so it's not until after it happens that I say I knew it."

Her father, also, "knew better and before I did—about sickness and about me. He didn't anticipate it hitting so close to home." It angered her father that he did not have precognition skills. "My father is more godlike with superpowers but I don't feel he's good. His energy is scary."

When asked how she could have stopped that sickness from ravaging the city, she said, "I should have known the pain it was going to cause and not allow it to happen." She felt her father was somehow the responsible party. "I knew he was going to do bad things. I should have stopped him. His needs ended up hurting people he loved. He cares only about himself. He uses others for his own personal gain. No respect for life. He's cold and unhappy. I'm different and he hates that part of me."

When I indicated I was confused about her statement, not understanding still how he or she could have been responsible, she added, "He IS the sickness. It originates from him. It feels like it was his actions but he didn't know it would have the effect on my mother or brother. His wanting power over people."

We never did ascertain whether this was a real plague or whether this was a metaphor.

Chris switched topics and said, "I'm sensing a very power-ful muscular horse." Speaking again as Bar, he added, "I liked riding the horse. I would ride to the ocean. The ocean was where I was most comfortable. He [father] wanted to keep me separated from the city. He wanted to control, but he didn't like the people in it. He didn't know about the rides. The kind old lady helped me to escape—go and come back undetected. He wasn't at home all the time—more concerned with whatever he did outside the home than in the home. He was greedy—always wanted more of anything."

Bar wasn't physically abused by her father, but added that the "abuse was more of neglect." As she grew older, their rela-tionship worsened and then, when she was 35, he disappeared. "Feels like he just left. He went away and didn't come back. Feels like I remained isolated after he left." [Chris said at this point he was feeling pain in his right shoulder.] "I was angry at him, at myself—mad at my mother. He goes out on a mission and never comes back. I don't think it was his choice to not come back." She believes he was killed.

Bar is set financially and says, "I don't have wants or needs. I spend a lot of time at the ocean and very little time in the city. I'm feared, not understood, and not welcome. For some reason I'm not comfortable with who I am. I'm different. I want to be normal so I don't accept myself for who and what I am. I feel much larger than everyone else. There is a very obvious physi-cal difference. It seems like I'm always looking down on them and they're always looking up. I want to be friendly and kind but they don't give me the opportunity. Because of my father they have a pre-conceived notion of who I am." Her mother and brother were "normal," and consequently more susceptible to whatever came through and killed them.

Bar dies by suicide, jumping off a cliff. She is in her 40s and is alone. She remembered being on the cliffs, looking out over the sea. "I love the ocean. I wanted to go back to where I loved. I dive off the cliffs. No real chance of surviving."

Her last thoughts were, "I don't want to play the role that I was supposed to play; carrying on my father's energy." She reasoned if she stayed alive she'd have to do that. "I never felt free. I resisted that part of me that was from him but I could never break free of it. It was always there. I thought if I wasn't chained to my body I could set my spirit free to be who I wanted to be—kind, light, majestic, free flowing. No rigidity, sternness, earthiness, meanness."

When asked if there was anything left unfinished in that lifetime, Chris said, "I don't think leaving the body left the things behind. It followed me into this life. I struggle with wanting to be soft and beautiful and free flowing and there are times when I am mean and angry and have no control over my mind and actions. I can't be loving all the time. Lot of physical pain, drug addiction, alcoholism, isolation, but that life wasn't the first time. I've been trying to get away and be different from that energy."

I asked Chris to think about his and Bar's life and explore any parallels or behavior patterns that are similar. "Even in this life, when I am on heights I scare myself because I have the urge to dive," he said. "I continue to isolate [myself]. Father in this life is still an evil man. Sickness, disease, horrible alcoholic. I'm a horrible alcoholic. I just don't drink [any more]. When younger, I drank and partied so I could die but didn't. I fell off a truck at 22 and landed on my face. I remember flying into heaven and that totally changed my desires. I'm still not

100-percent of who I am or was. Long recovery, work, healing, but I'm slowly becoming not what I used to be."

Chris's Soul Writing

Don't come down to their level. Be beauty. Be yourself. You have a choice. Know you are now for a reason. Love yourself. Be free. Have faith in your knowledge. Forgive. You don't need to hurt. Enjoy. Accept. Embrace your power. Pass the energy. Coyote. Horse. Love all. Mother. Don't be ashamed. Be proud. Trust us. Yourself. We forgive you. Don't be afraid.

In this life, Chris has not felt accepted, especially by his parents and his wife, none of whom have allowed him to be himself. Thus that sense that Bar had of being a misfit in society was rekindled in Chris's life.

Months after our session, Chris said no additional information came through for him regarding this lifetime, nor did he see the link between the pain that Bar felt and the pain he has experienced in this life. "I've felt [it] pretty much my whole life," he said, adding later that his feet and ankles hurt from childhood until recently.

In speaking about her father, Bar said her feelings toward him were "more fear than love; pain; hurt; no relationship." I asked Christopher if those feelings resonated to him in this life and if so, how were they mirrored in this life. He replied that his current father was never in his life. "I felt even more alone in this life."

Bar kept herself isolated and never left her family home mostly, she said, because her father did not want her to leave for fear of losing her. Yet she also said there was no love between the two of them. I asked Chris if those sentiments resonated with him toward anyone in his current life.

"I have put myself into relationships that were not great and loving, but stayed in them anyway," he answered.

As Bar, Chris said he had, "a wisdom or knowledge that I didn't trust. . . I get warnings from places . . . I don't think they're real." I asked him if that was a true statement for his life today. "I have heard warnings, but have not listened to them," he admitted. "The consequences have been severe."

When asked how Bar could have stopped the sickness from ravaging the city, she talked about needing to stop her father. She knew the pain he could inflict and yet she let it happen. She said her father hurt the people he loved; cared only about himself; used others for personal gain; had no respect for life and was cold and unhappy. She saw herself as different and because of that, her father hated her. I asked Chris if he could draw a correlation with any of these feelings Bar had with his present life.

"My father is the same way in this life," he said. "He doesn't hate me but it's hard for him to have a relationship because I don't drink."

He added that he continues to feel different and misunderstood in this life. "I've accepted who I am and don't care about others' opinions of me."

Writing in *Through Time Into Healing*, Brian Weiss addressed the correlation between suicide and past-life addictions. "Substance abusers who undergo past-life regression therapy sometimes discover that they have committed suicide in other lives and that the issues they wanted to escape from previously have resurfaced with a vengeance. This time the need to escape has been translated into the slower suicide and escapism of addiction."

In describing Bar's suicide, Chris said he didn't think leaving that body meant leaving the issues behind—that they followed him into this life. He said there were times he was mean and angry and had no control over his mind and actions. He pointed to physical pain, drug addiction, alcoholism, and isolation as all things he was contending with in this life, but he felt this was a pattern from multiple lifetimes. "I don't like the dark side of myself," he said. "I've worked very diligently to remove that part of myself."

Bar died from jumping off a cliff. Chris said in this lifetime that he was afraid of heights because he had an urge to dive. Knowing from our regression that feeling stemmed from Bar's life, I asked if that fear had dissipated any. "It's not a huge fear, but I can feel that feeling of flying to death," he said.

Each of his lifetimes focused on the same issue: that of self-worth, of free will, of the ability to choose behaviors and a path that led to ultimate freedom. Chris acknowledged he could see the pattern and that he definitely had self-worth issues in this life to the point of always wanting to satisfy others.

Chris said our past-life exploration impacted him in a positive way, in that his physical condition went away completely and he reported a spontaneous healing after our session.

Chapter Seven

Sexual Karma

The fires of the body
(Edgar Cayce Reading 272-4)

Some of the most powerful imprints that individuals bring in from previous lifetimes have to do with sexual promiscuity, molestation, or abuse—done either to or by the individual.

Edgar Cayce gave several readings attesting to this. One was for a 41-year-old housewife with what she called "a long history of emotional tension." She blamed part of that tension on the fact that her husband was impotent and for the last 18 years of married life, she had no physical connection with him. The arrival of a former suitor in her life precipitated an onset of health issues and she wondered if these issues were the result of her long abstinence or if it were karmic in nature.

Cayce gave her a life reading, saying that in one of her past lives during the Holy Wars, she was forced to wear a chastity belt because her companion did not trust her faithfulness in his absence. This did not go over well and in Cayce's words,

"This brought periods of disturbing forces of many natures; the determining to sometime, somewhere, be free, and to "get even." (2329-1).

She asked Cayce what were her obligations to her husband in this life and he responded: "These have been as problems ye have worked out together before. It was this companion who forced thee to be in that relationship during those periods of his journeys in other lands,—which has brought to thee the OPPORTUNITY for the meeting of same in the present" (2329-1).

While Cayce clearly attributed her condition to a previous life, he may not have known at that time how valuable a past-life regression would be to help her resolve that issue. Writing in *Through Time Into Healing*, Dr. Brian Weiss acknowledged how past-life therapy can be helpful in cases of abuse survivors—from any lifetime.

"Past-life therapy can be important to the healing process because for many adult survivors it provides a rapid, safe way of unlocking and clearing the experience, and because it also offers a large emotional and spiritual framework in which to process and integrate the memories that are released during the healing process. Past-life therapy gives victims new handles and hooks for approaching and grasping their experiences."

Never Stop to Strangle the Flow of Energy

Sean is a 50-year-old non-profit manager who described his chronic condition as urethral stricture near the perineum, i.e., an abnormal narrowing of the tube that carries urine out of the body from the bladder (urethra). He believed this was related to a previous life, or at least he was open to that possibility.

During his body scan he reported a burning sensation in the back of his foot toward his heels. In an unusual comment, he said he felt "gratitude" toward his legs and then reported having suffered twice with poison ivy on both calves. He envisioned his hips interchanging with female hips that were imposing themselves over his current male body. This would prove to be prophetic when we moved through the regression.

At this point, he saw a Native American woman and reported a kink in his hip joints. Not surprisingly, he felt a tingling in the perineum. There was tightness at the top of his heart, and a squeezing sensation between his shoulders and heart. At the bottom of his spine, he reported a soft, tender area in the sacral area, like a bruise, adding that his spine was a little twisted, but he felt no damage or sensitivity there. His right shoulder joint did not rotate correctly and his muscles tried to compensate. At first he said his neck felt fine, but then described choking at the base of his lower throat. He reported a stinging or burning sensation on his upper eyelids and said the top of his head felt inflamed and was pulsating.

Sean regressed to the year 833 in Palestine where he was a male in his 20s whose name sounded like "Balab." His body was similar to the one he has now, about 150 pounds, 5'7" or 5'8." His feet were covered and he wore what he described as work clothes, consisting of short pants and a sleeveless top made of a thick, leather-like material. He had thin, but muscular, arms and his hands were slightly work worn, with no cuts or callouses. His skin was light brown, as would be the complexion of someone from the Middle East. He had dark brown, almost black hair that was kinky, thick and curly. He chuckled that it would look somewhat like Bozo if he let it grow. He had a thick, full-trimmed beard that he said was "in good shape." He described his job as doing "physical work" as a blacksmith or leather smith, working under a canopy that was connected to his home. He lived in a dusty town with sandy dirt all around. Buildings were constructed of stone and stucco using very little wood, functioning as both commercial and residential properties.

He described his residence as something out of a Flint-stones cartoon—one room with small, uncovered holes in the walls as windows. His evening meal consisted of flat bread, egg-plants and onions served in a wooden bowl, then put on bread and eaten with hands. With him were his young wife, Sofia, and their son who was nearly two years of age. His wife and son both had dark hair. Sofia wore her hair in two long braids, one on either side. She had a darker complexion than his and a cheerful personality. "She was really happy," Sean said. "A lot of love between us." She reminded him of the character Mary Ann on the old *Gilligan's Island* television program. He felt very protective and close to his family but added that the word "love" did not adequately describe his feelings.

The significant event concerned an infidelity on Balab's part and the consequences of that affair. He was, "having a fun conversation with a young woman, 18, cute, sexy, playful in a mischievous sort of way. Feels like I'm having an affair with her. She has lighter hair and skin, large breasts, voluptuous. We start fooling around. Her skirt is on but her top is off. In the flash of an eye, she takes a knife out from the back of her skirt and stabs me in the crotch. Obviously she's very upset. We've been together in this way for less than a year. Might be during [wife's] pregnancy. It was obvious I would not be with her [the mistress] permanently. It's possible this was culturally accepted."

The injury was more embarrassing than life threatening. "She sliced the first quarter inch skin—not very deep but deep enough—same area as my surgery in this life," he explained.

"She sliced me to make her point. I pushed her aside, put a cloth between my legs and got out of there. I felt ashamed. How do you tell people what happened? It feels like I didn't tell anyone what happened. People don't see that part of my body. I may have asked someone for help. I'd like to think I could go to a healer or medicine person, but that feeling of shame is too strong to get past."

Later when Balab saw his assailant, she was with friends and they were smirking because they knew what she did to him. She never faced the consequences of what she had done because Balab was too ashamed to tell anyone. "I wanted to show them she missed, but I didn't do that, of course. My wife did see something happened but it doesn't feel like I ever told her the truth. She was very kind in taking care of me and healing the wound."

We discussed the present physical expression of this past-life incident and Sean said the doctors in this life said there was no reason someone his age should have those problems. "I still have shame to overcome," he admitted. "I led her on. It feels like I was an ethical guy. I wouldn't overtly make promises I couldn't keep. She was looking for a solid position. She may have had unspoken expectations. Just before it happened she was checking in to feel it out and I must have been joking. She came prepared. She made her point clear. She had no intention of killing me. She felt used."

Balab died in his mid-to-late 50s. He was lying on a granite table in that same house. His wife and several other people were there. "I feel cared for," he said.

Interestingly, the moment we began to discuss Balab's death, Sean felt a shooting pain at the base of his skull up to his brain. From this he perceived Balab might have suffered an aneurism or stroke. "It didn't kill me right away, but it was the beginning of the end."

His last thoughts were gratitude for his wife's love. "Not that I wasn't worthy—just grateful for the love and her sticking with me. Message to myself—love your wife!"

Sean said he and Balab share many similarities. "I have a strong, healthy body and a good passion for life. He's more serious than I tend to be. He's a good hearted man; capable of caring for his wife and child."

Sean's Soul Writing

Divine Mother, forgive us and let your love flow through me. Always be in me by me. Goodness lives in you. Allow it to flow. Never stop to strangle the flow of energy. Forgiveness is key. From the top of your head to the base of your torso, let it flow. Give of yourself and then receive. Like breath it goes in and out. Needs to be for life. In torso, out head. In head, out torso. Cleanse. Forgive. Flow. Love is pure life blue flame purifying. Let it flow.

My Soul Writing

In this life it is important for Sean to connect with people in truth and in trust. In the previous life he was a good person but was somewhat flippant about statements he made rather cavalierly. He thought he was saying one thing and was clear but it did not come out that way, nor was it heard the way he intended. This was an ongoing habit that eventually infuriated the young woman to the point where she could no longer take it and lashed out at him.

The physical condition in this life is a reminder to watch words and intent—to be clear, to be truthful. Then—as now—this soul naturally draws to it many other souls who are attracted to its energy, playful spirit and love of life. Remaining true is essential to maintain this love affair with humanity. Revealing the origins in several sessions will now act to release it—knowing origin, prayer and forgiveness will transmute the karma. It is not necessary to continue this pattern as he has included the law of grace in this life to transcend the karma from the previous life.

Sean did not experience any bleed through after our session. In reviewing his body scan, the only aspect he could connect to Balab's life was the tingling he felt in the perineum, saying he was stabbed in the same area. I asked if he saw Balab's act and subsequent injury as the karmic source of the physical issues he was dealing with today.

"Karmic? I suppose," he said. "I think of it more as holding onto the memory as an energetic pattern. My memory, mind, holding onto that intense emotional memory affects my physical body."

In reviewing Balab's life, Sean indicated there was a lot of shame to overcome. He mentioned this several times and then brought up feelings of guilt and shame associated with Catholicism in this life. I asked Sean if he believed there was a tie in between the shame Balab felt and the fact that he experienced and/or understood shame and guilt in this life having been raised Catholic.

"I believe so," he answered. "It makes sense to me that my soul chose my Catholic parents to create the right situation to bring this about and potentially heal it."

Sean said Balab's last thoughts were gratitude for his wife's love and for her sticking with him. He said the message to him was—love your wife. Since he knew from his own work that last thoughts often set up circumstances in the next lifetime, I asked how Balab's final thoughts impacted his present life circumstances.

"Hard to say, but I am still with my wife and I haven't had an affair!" he laughed. "His encouragement has helped on both fronts."

My soul writing suggested that in this life it is important for Sean to connect with people in truth and in trust, as Balab was less truthful and trustworthy than Sean is today. His physical condition serves as a reminder to watch words and intent—to be clear, to be truthful. I asked if he thought that was true and how Balab's infidelity and all that is associated with that was karmically impacting his life today.

"Good question," he answered. "I have been a pretty good 'boy scout' since I was a kid. Trust comes naturally because of my awesome parents and my faith. Being Irish and a people pleaser means that truth has been more difficult, but I don't think Balab's life is a huge influence there."

While his physical condition did not change as a result of our one session, he did give a resounding yes to my question about whether the session had impacted his life in any way, saying it helped him to see the light at the end of the tunnel.

The Smallest of Consequences Formulates Intent

Anne is a 40-year old health care professional who described her chronic condition as zero libido and painful intercourse. She only had pain-free intercourse a few times, and even less when it had been pleasurable. She was not in a relationship and felt this lack of libido and fear of pain was holding her back.

Anne was interested in participating in the project because she had known a few people who had significant changes in their lives after a past-life regression. She said she would be very happy if the same happened to her, adding that she admired and respected the work of Edgar Cayce. "A regression seems like a way to help heal myself, but also everyone else who came before me and those who are lined up to be next!"

She felt she was a good candidate because she was introspective and could tell the difference between messages from her rational brain, subconscious mind, and her body. "I also solidly believe that we are carrying shreds of experiences from the people we were before," she added. "While my baseline is mild skepticism, I've trained in energy medicine and am quite open to new ideas and possibilities."

Anne's body scan revealed discomfort in her left foot below her toes and tightness in her left quadriceps. She reported a cold feeling in her solar plexus. When we got to her shoulders, she had a sense that there was a wedge or divot in her left shoulder. Her neck felt as though it was being pulled to the left, as if the "whole structure is rubbery and bends to the left." She also complained of tightness running from the middle of her forehead to the top of her head.

Anne's regression introduced her to Brunt Kalder, who lived in 15th century England. He was short and in his mid-30s but felt older because he was worn out. His feet were bare and dirty. He wore ratty, droopy "hammer" pants with a low crotch and a shirt he described as merely a "random cloth on top." His hands were dirty and exposed. His sandy blonde hair was straight and mid-length, "not lush." Of his looks he said, "I'd be easily missed in a crowd."

Brunt described the landscape around him as hilly and rugged. He was on a stone road in a quiet town comprised of stucco buildings. There were wheeled carts in the marketplace and he recalled seeing a beautiful woman there, accompanied by several people who were nicely dressed. She would factor into his story later.

He ate his evening meal alone, hunched over a table in a dark, "not very cheery" room in his home. There was a big pot over the fire where he was cooking a stew, "something sloppy, but chunky." It contained basic ingredients and was "just good enough."

The significant event in this life occurred when he was an 8-year-old boy. He was happy, standing in front of a cart selling the apples, admiring the one in his hand. "The next thing I know I'm being kicked," he said. "A bigger kid came out of nowhere." He next sees himself and the apple lying on the ground. When I asked if anyone intervened, he replied, "Either no one is around or no one is doing anything about it. Then it stops."

He went home to his mother, which was the same place he described when having his evening meal, except at this earlier time it wasn't as dreary. He sensed a woman holding him and felt the presence of an apathetic father figure who withheld consolation. The father had his back to his mother and to him, almost disapprovingly. There was a fire in the hearth. A younger sibling, a sister around the age of two or three, was on the floor.

The beating caused structural damage and Brunt stopped growing. He eventually became hunched over. "I am made fun of over that," he said. "There is some pain involved for a chronic injury; the consequence of being kicked in the back."

Brunt returned to the memory of the beautiful woman in the marketplace. "She seemed new to the area, as if she were on vacation," he said. "She wasn't dirty. When I saw her and realized I wasn't like her, it wasn't a positive feeling. I don't know if it was predatory or not, more like, 'Oh look at that.' Resentment. The freshness she had was the trigger, a sort of, 'look how nice this is—a snapshot of life'—and I wasn't a part of that picture. Disdain. If she had seen me she wouldn't have liked me. I didn't look at life like that when I was a kid, appreciating then the freshness of the apple."

Brunt said his injury and the pain destroyed his childhood happiness and changed everything. His parents disappeared but he didn't say why. He didn't know what happened to his sister. He was alone. "I'm in pain and can't take care of myself; some sort of stigma around me. People are scared of me because I am misshapen and angry—more sadness because I can feel it now."

He did not see the woman again. "It's like silk that runs across your skin," he said. "It's gone but you can still feel it. She was a blip. Some negative feelings around her—not rape, but I wanted to hurt her because of what she symbolized. As a man not dating anyone, that would have been the case. It's worse to not have physical contact than know I could never be with her."

Brunt reported he was starting to get a sense of doing secretive things that weren't very nice, akin to slashing tires in this life, or tipping things over, with no one knowing he did it. Anne reflected on those feelings.

"Physically there is a lot of pain so it's hard to attack anyone, but at one point he saw a woman being raped and he watched," she said. "After it was over, he stood over the woman and didn't know if she was dead or not. It was more out of curiosity. He wasn't a psychopath or a terrible person, just someone with arrested development. Happiness turned into pain for good, so he never matured or developed emotionally. What he watched, he felt she deserved. Physical contact for him was not natural. He thought maybe that was the way she was used. He had no point of knowledge and his parents weren't models for him. He saw social contact as violent because of the way he was treated. He looked at her with curiosity and wondered whether that was what she really was for. She woke up and he ran off and did not tell anyone what he saw."

Brunt dies in his 40s. He accidentally was hit by something in the road and died instantly from blunt-force trauma and internal bleeding. His last thoughts were that his death was a huge relief. "I just wanted it to be done. Deep sorrow—no hope it would ever be resolved."

In comparing Brunt's life to her own, Anne said she has felt that no one sees or understands her; that she is in a lot of pain and no one cares. They don't reach out. While she admits these feelings have improved recently, she nonetheless was scary to approach in her younger years just like Brunt.

In terms of individuals from Brunt's life who are in her life now, Anne identified her present mother as having aspects of both of Brunt's parents. "There is the nurturing piece when there is an extreme, obvious need; otherwise, not as much. Sometimes there is dismissiveness."

When asked why she thought this life is the one her soul wanted her to see, Anne replied: "This person suffered a bully's injury—out of control. Not a reflection of his worth—it just happened. It may be a message I needed to remind myself of while I evolve with other people. Since a child I'd get physical sensations of being big and then it would go away. I've worked around that concept and energy. When I realized I wasn't that woman, that sensation came back. When I knew Brunt got kicked, that sensation went away. I wonder if it's a long time event that my soul decided needed to be resolved."

In terms of her physical karma, Anne said: "At the most basic level it's a sense of worth. Curious about the scene watching the rape, knowing I could never physically do that. Wonder if it was an intention I could never carry out? Symbolized my perturbed understanding of what connection was but it was violent. I realized that I could not go on. Over time, pain has gone away, but it's a dead zone."

My Soul Writing

Brunt is an interesting name as he was the "brunt" of bullying and later teasing and he received the "brunt" of the anger of this young bully. Interesting, too, is that the bully who kicked him mercilessly felt the same way about Brunt as Brunt felt about the woman in the marketplace. As a child Brunt was happy, enjoying life, admiring the beauty of the shiny apple—something that made the bully so jealous and angry—as he had so little and could not understand or relate to that joy—just as the woman loved life, the goods in the marketplace and Brunt was unable to relate to that anymore and that caused his disdain for her as the bully felt for him—and so it went full circle. The woman who was viciously raped—Brunt witnessed her pain as the act was done—thus he associated pain with intercourse and Anne brought that in with her—but only as a reminder of that life's bigger issues and lessons about interacting with others—something she is working on now. As these issue areas are cleared, she will get relief in all areas.

I discussed with Anne that Brunt's life was divided between who he was as a happy child up until 8, with who he became after the beating in front of the apple cart. I asked if she saw a similar dividing point in her present life—of the Anne she was up until one point with the Anne she became later.

"In hindsight I probably could identify my family's move out of state," she answered. "I was an awkward, yet clueless, happy fifth-grader when we moved. I had nice friends in Texas but felt very out of place because everyone seemed much more mature. By sixth grade, all the other girls were already shaving their legs and wearing mascara. Come to think of it, I was shocked to hear that a girl had sex with a boy in the bathroom. That shock has always stuck with me a little bit. We moved back before I started the seventh grade, but it all made an impression."

We discussed why Brunt kept going back to the memory of that beautiful woman in the marketplace. On the one hand, he admired her for her great beauty, but on the other, resented her and said her "freshness" served as a trigger, a reminder of all he didn't have. Anne thought he looked at life that way as a child— the freshness of the apple before the incident as opposed to after the incident. I asked her to expand on that idea and discuss how that was tied to her sexual issues in this life.

"I think I still look at life with a fresh perspective, trying to see the potential in all things," she said. "When I'm around people who aren't that way, I usually change my behavior to either become neutral or match their general mood. Both adaptations feel inauthentic and uncomfortable. It seems a parallel between that and sexual experience could be the vulnerability that comes with perceiving 'freshness.' Both sex and innocence are vulnerable states."

Anne said people were afraid of Brunt because he was "misshapen and angry" and that brought up tremendous sadness within him. I asked if the idea of being "misshapen and angry" ever came up in this life—even if in a different context—and if so did it cross into how she felt about herself in that it does not allow her to enjoy a sexual experience without pain.

"Sure!" she responded. "I have always had a problem with cystic acne and my skin is still plagued with shifting constellations of red bumps. That does sometimes make me feel both misshapen and angry. I might subconsciously link my appearance to pain during sex, but I'm not sure how that would be."

Brunt said he wanted to hurt the woman because of "what she symbolized" and Anne added, "it's worse to not have physical contact than know I could never be with her." I asked her to explain what those statements meant in terms of her past and present life.

"My guess is that statement was fueled by jealousy and resentment," she speculated. "Jealousy of her freshness—the innocent quality I used to cherish in the world—and resentment because she had it and I couldn't. An inability to feel like I was myself was likely the precursor to painful sex, because it prevented me from letting go and being vulnerable. On some level I certainly resent myself for not being able to just let go of things and be in the flow."

We reviewed her body scan and she felt certain that the cold feeling she reported in her solar plexus; the sense of a wedge/divot in her left shoulder; her neck pulling to the left; and possibly the tightness in her head, was rooted in Brunt's injuries.

In describing the rape Brunt witnessed, Anne indicated he watched more out of curiosity and then said, "What he watched he felt she deserved." She also said, "He thought maybe that was the way she was used," indicating he thought this may be the norm. Since rape is painful intercourse, I asked if she felt as though his silently watching this and not doing anything to help may have set up the condition she was dealing with today and she said that was entirely possible.

"I don't think it was the pivotal focus of this life," she added. "That was probably the injury and sense of betrayal. But, it certainly makes sense that it was a lesson that sex was associated with pain."

In discussing parallels of Brunt's life to hers, Anne said that what was similar was the idea that no one saw or understood her. She said, "I'm in all this pain and no one really cares." I asked how she thought that related to the painful intercourse issue she was dealing with today.

"Perhaps, if that's a deep-seated belief, it reaches to the core," she answered. "And the core would be that even during the most vulnerable, nurturing, primal time in life, I could be in pain without anyone noticing."

This was one of those lifetimes in which everything came full circle—that the bully who beat the "happy" Brunt could not understand or relate to that joy so he became jealous and angry and acted out of those feelings. The woman he admired loved life and the goods in the marketplace that Brunt was unable to enjoy or relate to and that caused his disdain for her just as the bully felt for him.

"That makes a lot of sense," Anne said. "It shone a light on the importance of sitting with emotions, especially extreme ones, to see where they're coming from. Some say we're angered or annoyed by people in whom we see traits that we dislike in ourselves. An introspective person might sit with these annoyances of others and wonder whether they might have that quality themselves. If they do recognize that and work to resolve it with themselves, they might prevent the lesson from having to be retaught in a next life and, in fact, save karma some time!"

Anne had no prior knowledge about her past-life aspect as Brunt, but said that overall, the session impacted her life in a positive way. "I'm usually not able to visualize or actively participate during energy work or hypnotism," she said. "The thrill of combining my imagination and intuition and knowing that I wasn't making any of it up inspired other creative thoughts that I've enjoyed incorporating into short stories and a novel that I'd started a long time ago. The entire process made me feel more empowered. Unfortunately, I haven't been able to test whether or not sex is painful anymore. . . but the moment the right guy comes along, I'll happily report back!"

Escaping Her Feelings

Debra is a 51-year-old registered nurse. She volunteered for the project to ascertain the origin of her Granuloma Annulare, a fairly rare skin condition that most commonly consists of raised, reddish or skin-colored bumps that are arranged in a circle or ring, usually on one's hands and feet.

During Debra's body scan, she complained of pain in the back of her left leg and said she occasionally felt pain in her upper hip area but not at that moment. She experienced pain every so often in her left breast and added she had a nickel-size birthmark beneath her right breast. She had a habit of biting the inside of her cheek since she was 5 years old, and had struggled with an upper range hearing loss since she was in her 30s.

Debra regressed to a life in 1717. There she saw herself as a young girl between the ages of seven and nine. She wore black leather pointed shoes and a cotton dress that was below her knees. She had light brown/golden hair that she wore in curls past her shoulders. A ribbon tied her hair back so it would not fall in her eyes. Her name sounded like Janine Sung.

Janine lived with her father in Cornwall, England in a two-story stone nobleman's cottage that was built high off the ground. They lived close to town, but there were no other houses within sight.

Her evening meal was taken on the second floor of that cottage in a large, multi-purpose room. The piano in that room provided, "the only fun thing I ever did." She sat on a bench at a table, eating a bland-tasting mutton and corn off fine china. Eating with her was her tutor, "someone to watch me," who sat on the other side of the table. He was in his 20s, thin, with dark hair. She said immediately that she did not like him.

The significant event in this life revolved around the two men who sexually molested her. The first was her tutor who molested her when she was between seven and nine years of age.

"He kept touching me and doing things to me," she said. "He would [do it] between lessons—not every time—a few times a week. He would make it part of a lesson to be a proper young lady. Inside I knew it was wrong. I didn't like it—made me feel terrible. I protested but he never listened. It went on for several years until he wasn't my tutor any more."

As a teenager, Janine was molested by her uncle who would come under the pretense of looking for her father. "He'd stay and smile at me." When I asked if the uncle raped her, she said, "He didn't penetrate—did everything but—he didn't want me to have a baby." She said she did not tell her father because she loved him and knew it would hurt him too much because he loved his brother, nor did she tell him about the tutor molesting her either.

When she was in her late teens, Janine married Stewart, a friend of her father's who was in his 30s. She described him as a kind and good man and said she didn't mind marrying him because she liked him well enough. They had two daughters together [as she has in this life]. When asked if the previous sexual experiences impacted her marriage, she said no. "At first with Stewart I was very uncomfortable when we were having relations, but he made me comfortable and I got used to it."

After a short illness, Janine died of pneumonia at the age of 70, surrounded by her family. Her last thoughts did not center on the molestation, but later she said she felt as though that issue was never resolved. "It was just there inside me. I kept it under and hidden."

In terms of parallels between that life and her present life, she said she wanted the same things in life then that she does now, i.e., family and love. In this life, she feels as if she has to "service" men. This goes back to when she was 18 and a virgin and her friends convinced her to help a guy get an orgasm. "I was high and felt it was my duty to help him." Later she had a boyfriend who told her that a friend of his would get beat up unless she performed oral sex on him.

"I was a good person in that life," she said, reflecting on Janine's life. "I was taken advantage of. I was not sexually abused in this life, except for one or two incidences that are not bad. When I was 8 years old, I played hide and seek. Some guys got me in a closet and touched me—stuff like that. Never bad. Never raped. Normal curiosity, exploration."

She is convinced that her insistence on keeping the molestation from the previous life inside is the cause of her rash in this life, attributing it to having those unresolved feelings. She hasn't met anyone she feels a romantic attachment to for 11 years and says that perhaps there is some resentment lingering.

My Soul Writing

Sexual molestation was common in that time period—more so than one would think. Since Janine had no mother and there were no females around, she had no role model and no one to talk to her about modesty or what was or was not appropriate male behavior. The tutor was sly and incorporated it into his lessons, so Janine felt it was all right—even though a part of her was uncomfortable. The uncle knew she would not betray him, as it would hurt her father. Despite the time, the fact that she kept this inside her—stuffed under her skin so to speak—it nonetheless impacted her. Today the same pattern exists—the keeping buried unresolved feelings. These need to be released. It is akin to building up a dam with water pushing against the sides. So great the pressure that portions seep through the crevices—like an infection seeping through pores of the skin. The skin condition—as with all physical karma conditions—is a reminder in the present time to not repeat the pattern from before. In this case it is unresolved issues—not all necessarily around sex—but other deeply buried emotions wanting to come to the surface but being suppressed. This can be resolved now. .. Understanding the root cause of the symptom is often enough to heal it.

In Debra's regression, she described the two significant events in that life as when she was sexually molested. In talking about the parallels between that life and her present life, she was convinced that keeping it a secret was the cause of her skin problems in this life.

"I've had skin issues in some fashion since I was a little girl," she said. "There is no history of that in my family. I just feel it is an 'eruption' of unresolved and repressed issues from a former life since it started before I was old enough to have issues in this one."

Debra indicated that in this life she had some similar experiences as Janine did with sexual molestation, even though she didn't think it was anything more than natural curiosity. I asked her to think about what Janine experienced and what she encountered in this life and determine whether that is what triggered the onset of the skin condition, even if it didn't manifest immediately. I asked if she saw that as a possibility.

"Yes, it is!" she said as if experiencing an ah-ha moment. "I had left a man I lived with for ten years, not being treated well and sexual problems were the main causes of that breakup. My current skin problems began within months of that time."

My soul writing suggested that Debra keeps buried unresolved feelings that need to be released, giving the analogy of a dam with water pushing against the sides—that the pressure was so great that portions of the water seeped through the crevices—like an infection seeping through pores of the skin. The skin condition, therefore, served as the reminder in the present to not repeat the old pattern—those deeply buried emotions that want to come to the surface that are being suppressed. I asked if she felt that was an accurate analogy when applied to her and her skin condition.

"I feel that is a VERY accurate description and I am hoping that my condition will improve as I resolve those feelings," she said. "My Granuloma Annulare condition causes me to have discoloration of my legs, which causes me to be embarrassed when I wear shorts or a bathing suit. I've had it on my arms in the past as well."

Debra said that the regression was very clear in her mind and that she felt like it was an aspect of her coming forth. "I felt the emotions of Janine and my intuition sensed certain things as well, like a 'knowing.' It was like I was there, part of sensing things and me knowing I was under regression but really feeling, seeing. When I was asked a question, I could hear myself talking almost like a 7 or 8 year old. I also could hear myself using expressions or saying certain things that I normally wouldn't as myself now."

When asked whether our session together impacted her life in any way, Debra gave a resounding yes. "Recently I was able to talk to my grown daughter about some of my issues in this lifetime. We discussed the regression as well and she helped me to 'get angry' about it. I am a very calm and passive person where I keep things inside and always seek forgiveness and love. She helped me to 'pound the pillow' so to speak."

Although her condition remained the same after the regression, Debra was optimistic about it changing in the near future. "I feel more resolved now and I am hoping my skin condition will soon improve."

Chapter Eight

Diabetes

"Affliction is God's shepherd dog to drive us back to the fold."
—Megiddo Message

The American Diabetes Association reports that in 2012, 29.1 million Americans, or 9.3 percent of the population, had diabetes, with the disease being credited in 2010 for being the seventh leading cause of death in the United States. With its numbers growing, it isn't surprising to learn that many suffering from this condition came to this project looking to see if its origin was from something they did in a previous lifetime.

Edgar Cayce gave readings concerning this condition and in 1925, he told a 53-year-old plant supervisor that his diabetes was the result of physical karma from his last incarnation during the witchcraft days in Salem, MA where he was: "... acting in the capacity of the executioner of the judgment as passed by the groups, or as "stool dipper" for those who did not adhere to the Puritan principles as set forth by the groups" (953-13).

Two volunteers came to my research project seeking the same answer. Sandra, who had suffered with Type 2 Diabetes since 2000, went back to a lifetime in 1811 New Mexico to find the origin of the imbalance in her life; and Janet discovered a life in 1650 Italy as the source of the stress she is repeating in this life that ultimately manifested as chronic fatigue that led to diabetes. Let's first look at Sandra's journey.

I Am Not of This Earth

Sandra is a 70-year-old retired community college professor who had quite a few past-life regressions over the years. The knowledge she gleaned from those sessions had been beneficial in helping her overcome challenges and work toward being a better person in this life. She hoped that searching her past lives for the cause of her diabetes and a hysterectomy she had at the age of 32, would help her advance toward a higher consciousness and level of spirit.

In her body scan, Sandra described numbness under the balls of each foot and at the front of each leg—more on the left between her knee and ankle. She felt emptiness where her uterus had been removed. She described something hard and round like a donut in her stomach, but she did not know what it was. She saw a black diamond-shape where the major veins enter the heart. She had the sensation of wearing two-inch wide, rigid bracelets on both wrists. In examining her spine, she described a strange shaping at the bottom from surgery.

Sandra identified her past-life aspect as Jacinto Muñoz, a slender, 12-year-old part-Mexican, part-Native American boy. Jacinto wore leather moccasins with non-descript beading. He had reddish-brown skin that was not very dark, and silky, smooth black hair worn in braids with a leather band around his forehead. He wore cuff-like, two-inch bracelets (which she picked up earlier in the body scan). He had on leather britches and a leather shirt with long fringe on the sides of his sleeves and his pants.

He described being somewhere in the southwestern United States, and by the looks of the cliff-like landscape, thought he may have been in Arizona or New Mexico. The only building he saw was a large family teepee with markings painted on it. "I'm wondering why there are no other people, but I'm not feeling afraid," he said. "I'm looking around, content. I like being alone—possibly I'm preparing for something. There's a fire pit but the fire is out."

At his evening meal, he is seated alone in front of a fire, but he is not eating. "I'm not supposed to be eating. I'm preparing."

In reviewing the significant event in his life, he described seeing a member of his tribe on horseback. The rider held a spear adorned with feathers in his left hand.

"He's riding toward me and I am just looking at him," Jacinto said. "I don't feel fear. He comes charging toward me. Still no fear. Waiting. I think it's a test of some kind but I am not sure what I am supposed to do. He thrusts the spear into my abdomen and I fall to the ground. He stops, turns his horse around and looks down at me. I smile at him. He smiles back and rides off, leaving the spear in my abdomen. I sit up and look at it. I don't feel pain but feel drugged and in a fog, probably because of the peyote I had smoked beforehand as part of the ritual. I pull out the spear and want to hold my shirt over the wound, but that won't work because the spear goes through my shirt, so I take off my moccasin and press that over the wound. I sit there holding it, wondering what to do next. Out of nowhere an older woman comes rushing over. She's upset and is fussing over me and has the other braves carry me into the teepee. I thought I was alone but they were closer than

I thought. I'm smiling because I didn't die. I am proud I passed the chief's test. If you survived this you were worthy and meant to lead. If you died, you weren't meant to lead."

Jacinto next saw himself as a grown man, wearing a huge headdress with feathers going down his back and a heavy-weight champion-like belt. His muscular legs were bare and he was wearing a loincloth. He stood at the front of a temple on a mountain. Sandra said he had been groomed for this position from the time he was a young boy because by not dying he was special. "It's not a fancy Indian temple," she explained. "It's at the mouth of a cave with carvings on it. It's manmade. I'm a medicine man—a shaman."

It was at this point that his name changed to White Eagle. "After I passed the shaman test at 12 and healed myself, I was given the name of White Eagle by The Old Ones on the other side in a vision. White Eagle is not, and never has been, a generic name. Was I a famous White Eagle? I have no idea. I had no knowledge of what was happening in other parts of the world or of what people thought of me. I knew only my spirit-filled world of the cave and the beauty of nature beyond. I did what I could to help all creatures of the earth."

White Eagle spent most of his life alone. "People came to me for help but I didn't interact with them," he explained. "It has to do with the smoke. It's not incense. It's used to cleanse the temple cave and to keep me in a state of readiness to talk to spirit. Long-term usage of living in this has something to do with my present condition."

Sandra said the spear to the abdomen marked the same spot in this life where she underwent an emergency appendec-tomy. "In that life that is what saved me," she said. "The spear hit my appendix and that kept me from being further injured."

Sandra believed strongly that her chronic condition in this life related to the smoke White Eagle kept going all the time, enabling him to be in a constant drugged high. "That's what shamans used," she said. "They related that with connecting to spirit, helping you go into a trance-like state to get information. Whether I chose to burn it all the time or learned to do that, it was my way of being ever prepared. If I'm always in this state I can help right away. However, it did wear down my body and its functioning and shortened my life."

She believes that smoke seeped into her system and she carries that with her to this day. "In this life it is making me lethargic and affecting my blood sugar," she said. "I feel as though it is still filling my system and I need to get it out so my system will work properly again."

Interesting to note that when she first discovered she had diabetes, she described that it felt as though she was walking into a heavy wind and couldn't move forward. "That fog has followed me and filled me and shut down my insulin mechanism and I need to get rid of the fog to get my body to work properly."

Jacinto died alone in the cave at the age of 35. He attributed the cause of his death to the smoke. "I just went to sleep and didn't wake up."

His last thoughts were, "Peaceful—okay—now I go to the other side. Close with the other side—spent so much time with the other side—not much of a transition."

Looking at parallels between the two lives, Sandra said, "I like being alone in this part of my life. I enjoy helping people. I'm wiser now so when people ask me for wisdom, I am grateful and eager to give it—that matches Jacinto. He was better at calling to the spirits than I am. That smokiness he felt around him I am feeling more. I seem to be in a fog more than out of it.

Haven't used it to the good. Fog—not confused by lack of focus, self-discipline to do what's best for me. Easier not to do it. Focus and self-discipline go hand in hand. Unless I can take control it will get worse. Jacinto began confusing reality and spirit of when he was in other world, which is why he didn't mind dying."

Sandra's Soul Writing

I am White Eagle. I AM White Eagle! I come from a long line of healers. I was taken from my family, my home immediately after my birth so I would have no earthly attachments. My family is spirit. Mother Earth. Father Sky. The Old Ones. They are my family. I am related to no one on earth. I am here only to serve the people. To help them, to guide them, to heal them. I live my life in my cave/temple. I greet the morning sun. I see the moon to sleep. I am one with them—one with the seasons, one with the weather. I am not of this earth. I am the channel, the gateway to the Wise Ones. I seek the truth. I do not let man's petty emotions and arguments affect me. Those are of no consequence. Only the higher truth is important. All must walk the path—but many stumble and lose their way. The right path is obscured by fog, by anger, by jealousy, by hate—so they follow the only path they see—the wrong path. Why do they not return to the good path? They get so caught up in the physical—they do not take the time to focus—to clear their minds—to see where they are, where they are headed, and where they need to be. I cannot help them find the right path. I can aid in the search, but I cannot create the will, the drive that is needed to lead them there. That is all. Aho!

About a month after our session, Sandra reported receiving additional insights in meditation. "I saw the beauty of a peaceful meadow with a waterfall and stream overtaking (like Kudzu) a dark, barren world. I interpreted that as a cleansing of my body, clearing out the smoke and replacing it with health. I see water as a large part of the cleansing process."

In the regression, Sandra described Jacinto as someone who liked to be alone. I asked whether that sentiment resonated to her in this life.

"Since 2000, when I was diagnosed with Type 2 Diabetes, I have enjoyed being by myself more and more," she said. "As the 'smoke'/diabetes takes over my body, I become more like Jacinto. My mind and body and spirit are out of balance; my life is out of balance. To return to health, I must return to balance in all areas of my life. Hence, a need for cleansing."

Jacinto had to pass an important test—the spear in his abdomen—that Sandra said was a chief's test. I asked whether she associated the need to be tested to suggest her worthiness in this life and how that attitude tied in with her present life.

"I have always tested myself in this life," she said. "I have always set my own rules and my own goals. In my mind, success in life equals making money equals worthiness. When my son was young and I was not working, I definitely felt unworthy—maybe not quite worthless, but close. Now that I am retired, I feel worthy of a good life based on my accomplishments during this life."

Sandra mentioned that the location of where the spear entered Jacinto's abdomen was the same as where her appendectomy was in this life, adding that the spear connecting to the appendix is what saved Jacinto's life. I thought that was a rather remarkable tie-in and she agreed.

"I find it interesting," she said. "When I was in the fifth grade, I complained about severe pain in my abdomen for several days. My mother said I was eating too much. Finally, she took me to our doctor, who immediately called a surgeon to schedule an emergency appendectomy. Since Jacinto's appendix was never removed and the smoke in his system masked any problems, I think the need for its removal manifested in this life."

Sandra said in this life the "smoke" was making her lethargic and causing issues with her blood sugar, as if she still sensed the smoke was in her system. I asked her to elaborate what she meant and how she felt it was still impacting her.

"The smoke equals the excess sugar in my system, slowing down the processes of my mind and body, making my brain 'foggy' and leaving my body without energy. In the last week or so, however, my blood sugar numbers have come down to a more manageable level. My brain is becoming clearer, but I still have little energy."

Staying on that theme, I reminded her that when she first discovered she had diabetes, she said she felt as though she were "walking into a heavy wind—couldn't move forward." She added, "That fog has followed me and filled me and shut down my insulin mechanism and I need to get rid of the fog to get it to work properly." I asked her to elaborate on what she meant.

"I think the interpretation is that I need to clear my system of my past emotions and experiences so I can move forward," she answered. "I must cleanse my body, my mind, my life of all negative influences and unnecessary distractions. Those actions will set my spirit free to fly higher and closer to The One so I can achieve my maximum potential."

Sandra did not see much of a tie-in with Jacinto's life and the body scan we did, with one exception. She identified

Jacinto as asexual, with no interest in women one way or the other. In the scan she identified emptiness where there was no uterus and after the session said that might possibly represent her need to return to an asexual state of being. I asked how that translated into her present sexuality.

"I should have said, 'no interest in women OR MEN,'" she answered. "There was no connection to anything earthly . . . only to the sky, the sun, the moon, the stars, the weather, the spirits. Wait. My only connection was to the white eagle, which brought me messages from the people. In this life, as a child, I saw the powerlessness of women and didn't want to be one. I was a tomboy and challenged the boys in any way I could. I would lead the girls against the boys in games on the playground. I told everyone I never wanted to get married. I must have been quite forceful about it because my grandmother, who made a full-sized quilt for all her grandchildren, made a single-sized one for me!"

Sandra knew nothing about Jacinto being one of her past-life aspects until we did the regression. Yet even before we got into that life, she was dealing with issues about "smoke" or "fog." During the regression induction when I asked her to walk up a stairway, she said everything was foggy as if she were walking inside a cloud. She somehow found the door leading to Jacinto's life, but again said she was surrounded by fog and could see nothing when she walked through the door.

"When you asked me to look at my feet and describe them, I could not see through the fog," she said. "I thought the regression wasn't working. I was starting to panic. I kept staring hard at the fog to see if I could get through it. Then it slowly began to clear, and I began to describe my moccasins and clothes. I felt relieved and I could relax and continue on my journey."

The soul writing was especially poignant for Sandra. She said it came easily to her and that the words flowed from her mind onto the paper. It ended quickly with, "That is all. Aho!" Sandra said that was because that aspect of her that is White Eagle was finished speaking. "He was doing the writing, not I," she said. "It gave me a clear understanding of White Eagle's perspective on life's purpose. Seeking the higher truth. Clearing the mind and focusing on the current path. Assessing the situation and returning to the good path."

Overall, the regression/soul writing session gave Sandra a clearer understanding of her current physical and mental conditions and ways to improve them. While her condition did not go away completely, it did improve substantially.

A Lack of Sweetness in Life

Janet is a 54-year-old marketing professional that I had worked with before in my previous research project. In that session we were able to decipher that her chronic fatigue was rooted in a previous life, but at the time we did not explore it further. When she indicated she suffered from both chronic fatigue and diabetes, I wondered how the two were connected. Janet felt strongly that her blood sugar levels were driving the fatigue.

"The last regression I had with you I learned a tremendous amount about myself and the pattern this life has followed from my past life," she said. "There are changes I want to make in this life so that I do not repeat the same learning lessons. I believe if we recognize our patterns we have a chance to change them. I am trying to be diligent in changing my life from what I learned in my last regression. Since then a lot has happened in my life. Randy, my fiancé of eight years, died at 49. I gave up our house and pets, and have gone on the road for a sales job in two states. My company may be selling to another company so I am still reinventing my life. My hope is to meet a potential husband and work in the health industry doing something that allows more time at home to have a fuller life outside of just working."

Janet's method of processing was unique in that during the body scan, she identified chronic conditions by color. When we started with her feet, she said she had a bunion and cut on her right foot, accompanied by corns and toughness. She saw a yellow/green color swirling on her right foot and said the bottom of her foot was gray. She heard the words "walk," "rocky," "barren," and the phrase "skeleton bone." She asked herself whether she made them tough with her mindset.

She saw a maroon red/purple color around her ankles and said that purple was her pain color. Her knees had more of a yellow color and started to bother her when we got to that part of her body. She saw herself crawling in the dirt, over a rocky, barren landscape. "Yellow at the knees could mean that they have lost that vibrant feeling—green turns yellow when losing its life force. Is it that I am stuck and not moving forward?"

When we approached her reproductive system, she reported having a uterine cyst, but added that this was more an intellectual assessment than what she saw. However, she added that she could see a dark black color inside the uterus. "Black is about a murky, clogged area," she said. "I know that I have a small uterine cyst so I may have thought about how cysts block/wall off poisons. Am I not birthing my soul's purpose?"

Navy blue surrounded her kidney and she equated that with fear. There was a lime green outline around her bladder. "Do I not see the crystal clear blue of my dreams and instead see the lime green acid eating away my life's purpose?" she asked. "Bladder lime green acid—pissing away my life. It is not too late to have the crystal blue clear waters?"

She reported tightness in breathing but thought it had to do with the removal of her gall bladder. Her intestines were brown and her lymph nodes were yellowish orange. "Yellow/ orange lymph system: will walking my true path clear up the yellow (lack of vitality)? Orange-decaying lymph system?"

Going into her chest, she saw pink and white and identified that as love surrounding her heart and lungs. "Pink is a symbol of love and white is purity and reflects all colors. So if I follow my heart, take a deep breath, and make things easier life will become much happier and not such a struggle for me? I could experience the fullness of what life has to offer." She also saw a scar in the heart area and said the pain she reported earlier in her chest had dissipated and she could breathe easier.

There was a small scar on her right hand and she reported seeing royal blue around her wrists that ached slightly. "Blue at my wrists could be my working a lot and cutting off circulation," she said. "Need to work smarter, not harder, putting hands to good use, accomplishing my purpose and not doing needless, repetitive tasks that are not what I am here to accomplish in this lifetime."

Janet saw ashy contrasts around her spine and it made her jumpy when I instructed her to go up and down her spinal skeleton looking for discomfort or sensitivity. She reported her nerves as overactive. "Spine—feeling like I am in overdrive. When I look at it I want to accomplish more easily but not wear my body out in accomplishing my purpose for this life. I am currently on the road traveling for someone else's dream that is wearing me down. Hoping to get my lessons quicker and move on without staying stuck and wearing myself out.

I want to manifest my life's purpose to the highest good with ease and grace."

There was discomfort radiating to her left thumb, making her uncomfortable. She saw a purple/royal blue outline there, again indicating pain. "Left thumb radiating pain represents not spending enough time with my yin feminine self. I am the sole support in my life so I tend to use a lot of my yang male side for work so I feel I may need to nurture my feminine yin."

There was blue around her neck. "Blue in neck is probably about cutting off my voice and what I want out of this life."

When we examined her head, she began touching each eyebrow and said that there was a scar on her eye even though she wasn't seeing or feeling it. "I feel the least in this area—maybe in my jaw a little tightness." She later said the tightness in her jaw was the clinching she did to get through each day. "I may block some of the feeling so I can continue to move forward providing for myself, doing something that I do not see right now, how it is in alignment with my life's purpose. I do see how my current experience will be of great benefit for what I believe is my life's purpose. Each step I have taken has greatly prepared me for the next step. It is amazing how events unfold in your life that propel you forward for the next step."

Janet's regression took her to the year 1650 in Italy. She described herself as a middle-aged Caucasian woman by the name of Jaclyn Connor. I thought that was an unusual surname for an Italian lifetime, but then surmised it could have been her husband's name, as he originally was from England.

Jaclyn was tall and thin, with long, slender and well cared for hands. She wore natural-colored slippers. Her mossy green long dress had a white cream-colored hem. The dress was made of lesser quality silk and was folded, curtain-like, on the right side. Her silver-ringlet wig was worn under a "tacky" hat that matched her shoes. Janet wasn't sure if Jaclyn made her clothes or bought them. She had money and kept wondering why she was wearing that dress, saying it did not match the value of the house she was seeing.

Jaclyn lived in a hilly, barren and dry area that was not at all like the green area she was standing on. Wherever she was, she felt out of place. She described one-story brown houses with clay flat roofs. The doors were unusual in that they went up and around and had no windows. She lived in a two-story home that was beautifully landscaped and nicer than the others, but added that wasn't the norm. She said the inside of the house did not fit with what she saw on the outside.

Jaclyn's evening meal was taken with her husband Henry, who was wearing an all-gray outfit that Jaclyn had selected and placed on the bed for him to change into when he came home. He had on knee-high striped dark gray britches, black stockings and a dark hat. Henry was around her age and had dark brown hair that was showing some signs of gray.

Their meal consisted of some type of gruel mixed with very little meat, with potatoes, a grain of some sort, and carrots—no greens. They ate off pewter dishes while sitting on a bench at a long, plain wooden table that was not what you'd expect in an upscale home. They used very plain, rustic silverware.

When asked about their relationship, Jaclyn said, "We're not as connected as we should be. We're going through the motions." There were no children. "I'm getting the feeling her husband was a good man and worked hard to get all they had," Janet added.

When we discussed the significant event in that life, she said Henry was tired and she didn't understand why. Janet had a feeling that Jaclyn could be better to him. "She had a lot of energy and wanted to do things and he was tired. She wasn't appreciative."

At this point, Janet said her thoughts could not get away from thinking about the landscape, adding that the house wasn't very plush and that Jaclyn wasn't working but wanted more so Henry worked all the harder. "She can't get content and happy," Janet said of Jaclyn. "She has an attitude of entitlement."

Jaclyn had seven siblings. Her family did well but she did not get much attention. "It looked like they were doing okay, but lacked love," Janet said. "As a child she wore white. She believed outward appearances made it all right. She didn't get love as a child so she can't give it to her husband. There is a lack of sweetness in her life. I get a feeling the lack of sweetness and love came from her parents. The siblings acknowledge each other but it's surface stuff."

Henry Connor was a blacksmith by trade and came home smelling from smoke and fire. He worked hard to have the house and the money to take care of her. He was creative and did well. He put in long days and wanted to relax when he came home, but she insisted they dress up.

"She didn't experience hard work or that feeling like he did," Janet said. "I know his feeling. It was not dishonorable work, just hard. There was a lack of love in that household. She didn't know how to love him because of her childhood, but he thought being with her was happiness."

Janet began questioning whether Jaclyn was with Henry for what he could provide in terms of attention and material objects. "She was trying to fulfill her contentment from outside and saw him as a way to do this," Janet said. "She has no friends. She's not struggling financially—she's starving emotionally. She's starving him emotionally as well. The man is tired. He married her because she came from a better background. The thought was—you have to work hard to do well. He can't figure out how to give her the sweetness. He doesn't know what else to do for her. She doesn't demand more but doesn't want to totally love him. There is no physical connection. They just go through the motions—no spark. She just makes meals and looks pretty."

Janet continued to be perplexed about Jaclyn's attire and said there was some confusion about why she was dressed up. "She didn't go anywhere," she said. "Just dressed up and was in the yard waiting for him. He cleaned up for dinner with her. She picked out the outfit he wore to the table. He does it for her. He does a lot for her. These things don't matter to him. He could have a simple life. They aren't congruent together. Henry is very content. I don't know if she'll ever be content."

Jaclyn dies unexpectedly at age 55. She is in bed in a second-floor bedroom. There is a window to the right of her bed and she is wearing white nightclothes. Henry is in the house but not with her at the time of death. "She had a fever from the flu," Janet explained. "I got the impression her family believed she wouldn't die. She dies while he is downstairs making soup."

Jaclyn's last thoughts were that she wished she could have done it differently—to be happier and more content. She regretted not being more loving to Henry. She just could not get passed "the stuff."

Janet reflected on the similarities between Jaclyn and Henry, and her life with Randy. "When I was with Randy before he died, I should have been more grateful for what he did," she explained. "I should have saved money. I was given chances to do better but didn't do it. I feel you have to work hard to do well. Dad's family all has diabetes and there is a lack of sweetness in his family. There is a pattern of needing to work hard. I should have been better toward what I have and be more appreciative in relationships I'm in today. Parallel—allow love and sweetness—you don't have to work so hard to have the sweetness."

Randy died suddenly, just as Jaclyn had done, and like Jaclyn his relatives were not there because they thought he'd live. Janet thinks they reversed roles. "It's about love, heart, being with people. Not about houses, cars, clothes."

I asked Janet how any of this related to her present physical condition and she said that the fatigue and overachieving in this life makes her blood sugar spike due to stress. "Chronic fatigue cascades down to diabetes," she said. "Stress in family intertwines with diabetes."

Janet's Soul Writing

Lessons.

Love.

You have all you need now.

Family, friends

Relatives.

Not about stuff.

Be what you want to feel.

It does not have to be so hard (life).

You make it hard with thoughts.

You are enough—have enough

Can be enough.

Not the outside—inside.

Little can be a lot.

Enjoy the moments now.
Now is all we have.
Do not overdo—for what?
Enjoy the smallness of life—nature.
Nature is beauty.
Jaclyn outside in beauty of
Landscapes (nature)
Henry—ashes—hot—tiredness
Having to provide extra.
Few nice clothes, not lots
Overwork=overtired=lack of contentment, love—life.
Lack of sweetness—short-lived life.
You want life well lived.
Fear of future stops us from enjoying today.
What about today?
Henry took everything upon himself
to provide happiness for someone else.
Provide happiness for self/other?
Be happy, grateful!!

My Soul Writing

Janet used one word, "sweetness," many times—a term aptly used to describe the diabetes in this life. She had no sweetness then. In this life she fights to control her blood sugar—too much sweetness. So it is a complete reversal—except the sweetness then was an attitude and not a physical condition. So too is there a reversal of where an attitude turns into a physical condition in her attitude toward her husband. Jaclyn lacked compassion and understanding toward her

202

husband's fatigue due to his hard work, so it is in this life she experiences chronic fatigue due to her own hard work.

Janet reported significant bleed through after our session and was convinced that Jaclyn's lifetime was a big lesson for her in this life. "Learning to appreciate the simple things in life and not want things that require you to stress yourself and you end up too tired to enjoy them," she said. "Happiness can be obtained by simplifying your life. I am in the process of cutting out things that stress my life so that I can experience the happiness I desire in this lifetime."

Janet repeatedly made reference to the fact that Jaclyn "lacked sweetness" in that life and yet in this life, Janet suffers from diabetes, an overabundance of sweetness one could say. I asked her to discuss the tie-in between the two and what she learned as a result of the regression in terms of her present condition.

"Diabetes is said to come when there is not enough sweetness in your life," she said. "So, the body over produces sugar to compensate for the lack of sweetness. Jaclyn had a lack of sweetness in her life because she could never get enough. This lifetime for me has not been easy. I need to see the sweetness in nature and the simple beauty of this world."

We also discussed the fact that Jaclyn had little sympathy for how tired her husband was, and in this life Janet suffers from Chronic Fatigue Syndrome. I asked her to elaborate on how those two fit together.

"Due to my fatigue I can only do so much and I have to stop," she said. "I no longer can push the envelope for more and more. I do not have the energy to enjoy things when I am tired. Chronic fatigue may have come to teach me the lesson of how Henry felt when Jaclyn pushed him to work hard to provide more and more material things. The lesson could be two fold: showing me how Henry felt in that lifetime and that never being grateful for what you have can make you too tired to enjoy anything else."

Janet believed strongly that Randy had been Henry in her previous life. In terms of karmic conditions, or repetition of patterns, I asked her to discuss those similarities in more detail.

"Randy worked very hard to have more and more beautiful things," she said. "I kept telling him we could simplify and not work so hard and enjoy life. He never took much vacation and worked more than one job. In the end I feel the stress and lack of taking good care of himself was the cause of his early death. Jaclyn also died an early death. Randy and I seemed to reverse roles from our past life. Jaclyn loved the yard and landscape. Randy found stress relief in the yard and was known to have a beautiful landscaped yard that he did himself. Randy was a very good carpenter as well. He was very creative. That aspect was more like Henry but Henry could enjoy simple things. Randy enjoyed being home but like Jaclyn, he had to have a certain home with certain things in a really nice neighborhood. When I suggested that Randy downsize and move to make things easier he said, 'I will die in this home before I move.' He did die in his bedroom at the age of 49."

In her soul writing, Janet wrote in verse, some of which was quite profound. I asked her to elaborate on what those phrases meant in terms of both Jaclyn's life and hers.

"I need to be happy every day and enjoy my journey," she said. "I have what I need every day. I need to learn how to live life doing what I love and not what I think I have to do to survive. My thoughts about how hard life is keeps me stuck. I can manifest what I want with the right mindset. Be grateful for nature and the small beautiful things we often are too busy to notice. Being always worried about tomorrow does not allow us to enjoy the journey or be present in the now. Really all we have is now. I would like to create my life in the now. Be what you want to feel means to be loving and caring and you will feel loved and cared for yourself."

Janet had no idea that Jaclyn was one of her past-life aspects and was surprised at how clear she saw images from that life.

"Everything seemed to come to me as the questions were asked," she said. "The pictures would pop into my mind and the thoughts would immediately follow. The regression had the same theme throughout. My life will be happier and easier in this lifetime if I would just simplify everything that I am trying to accomplish. I currently have too many projects and interests going on in my life, which keeps me fatigued and that stops me from being able to accomplish my life's purpose."

Janet said the session impacted her life in a positive way in that she began the process of becoming more intentional with her life's purpose.

"Simplifying things is opening doors to accomplish what I really want and saying 'no' frees up time to do the things that really make me happy. I get what is important now!! I have been trying to clarify my health-coaching niche. Is it dealing with stress and chronic fatigue clients? This seems to be my lesson in this lifetime. It would be a way to help others with similar issues in this lifetime. I have spent over half my life working on these issues for myself."

Janet's chronic condition did not go away completely, but she reported that it had improved substantially after our session.

"I believe that recognizing the root cause can help you begin to alleviate your health problems," she said. "I have a different mindset on how I am approaching my life. This will reflect in more happiness (diabetes relief) and less fatigue (chronic fatigue). My mind can let the overly burdening things go and life can be lived with ease and grace. Simplifying my life will change how I feel every day. This is such a valuable lesson that I could not clearly see until my regression. I will always be grateful."

Chapter Nine

Emotional and Mental Disorders

"For each soul meets itself in that phase of its experience in which the errors occurred that bring the results or effects in the present."
(Edgar Cayce reading 3511-1)

"Of the mental disorders, depression, suicidal tendencies, and multiple personalities, along with certain other forms of schizophrenia, seem in some cases to be past-life related," writes Glenn Williston and Judith Johnstone in *Discovering Your Past Lives, Spiritual Growth through a Knowledge of Past Lifetimes.*

That certainly was the case with my last two subjects. As with alcohol and drug addiction, I did not want to work with individuals with emotional or mental disorders, as generally they do not make good subjects for hypnosis. However, both Angel, who has bipolar disorder, and Irene, who experienced recurring night terrors, were nurses and the detail in their past-life recall made them exceptional subjects.

Could See I am Whole

Angel is a 57-year-old registered nurse who had two past-life regressions prior to volunteering for my research project. The first was a group regression in which she saw herself as a large, muscular, chained black African slave on a boat heading to the United States. Her second regression occurred after the birth of her second child when she had what she called "a mental breakdown." When she was brought to a hospital emergency room bathroom, she saw herself in Salem, MA during the height of the witch trials, a theme that comes up repeatedly among healers doing regression work. Despite the fact that they did not burn witches in Salem, she nonetheless believed the common myth that this was true and was fearful she was going to be burned. "I started overflowing the bathroom with water," she said. "They had to break down the bathroom door to turn off the water."

She came to me after being diagnosed with bipolar disorder for which she was taking many medications. In the initial body scan she identified a tingling at the bottom of her left foot and side of her right foot. Her right knee was uncomfortable and her right groin area tender. She felt tightness in the band around her waist and dullness around her heart. She said her arms felt like thorns on flowers and her shoulders ached as though she was carrying a big heavy bag on her back. When we got to her throat she said she felt a need to yell but did not have the voice to do so. She also said she felt a tightness in her lower jaw.

During the regression, Angel went back to the year 1492 in the Celtic Isles. There she saw herself as a 40-year-old tanned male named Xavier Moss. He was average height and weight, with hairy arms and well-groomed hands. He was balding, and had a mustache and a reddish-brown beard shaped in a "V." He wore gold shoes that were curled up at the toes, and a one-piece maroon and gold striped garment consisting of a shirt and pantaloons secured with a belt. Angel said he felt like royalty. Xavier's two-story, rectangular country home was made of red stone and had many white windows.

His evening meal was taken in a banquet hall at a long table surrounded by many chairs. He was dining on what he described as "a big animal." Although they had crude utensils made of wood, he ate off fine china. His family sat at the table with him. His wife, Vivienna, was dressed in black and had something over her head. Xavier said she always dressed that way.

The significant event revolved around Vivienna, who was suffering from what we would now identify as depression. "She feels distant," Xavier said, adding that although they were married, they had no relationship. There were four children at the table, including three teenage boys and a 7-year-old girl. The oldest boy looked like Xavier and was very outgoing, learning how to manage the estate. The middle boy was intelligent, but quiet and interested in books. The younger boy stayed below the radar and felt somewhat lost, with minimal connection to the family. Xavier described the girl as full of love, light and energy—the direct opposite of his wife.

Xavier said Vivienna's condition had been like that from the early part of the marriage. He had tried everything, including herbs, to help her feel better but nothing worked.

"She had the children when she was really young," Xavier said. "With each child, she became more depressed and dysfunctional. She is withdrawn and stays in her room, only coming out for meals. I put a wall up between her and me because I don't know what else to do. She doesn't know how to get better. There is no thought to divorce. She's like one of the children. I'm disappointed. I see other people who are married and have a good life and I don't have that. But I have a commitment. It feels like I should stay."

Xavier felt as though he were split in two—trying to handle a 300-acre estate and his family at the same time. He identified himself as a nobleman who relied on servants to do the cooking and cleaning, but did not employ a nanny. People expected to be invited to his home but he couldn't have dinner parties because of his wife's condition.

Xavier admitted he resented her because she wasn't "the person I married." He also admitted to feeling lonely, having only his brother to talk to. Most of his time was spent at home because he had "lots of responsibility just managing the estate." There was a nearby village, but he couldn't get there often because he was too worried about his wife and all that he had to manage. In contemporary language, he described his situation as being, "kinda stuck."

His wife died seven years later. "She whittles away to nothing," he says. "The children are grown now. They never had a bonding with their mother so it's a death with no sadness because she's been dead a long time emotionally."

Xavier follows his wife in death shortly after. He is 47 at the time and describes lying in a large, dark bedroom decorated in red brocade wallpaper. His oldest son is with him. He dies of a liver problem that Angel believes was hepatitis. His last thoughts were that he now had freedom from all that tension. He can relax and let go. "It was a hard life," he said. "It wasn't easy because of her and that time period. People got sick with no doctors. Even as a nobleman it was a lot of work."

In reflecting on Xavier's life and her current life, Angel felt she had taken on the role of Vivienna in this life and that her ex-husband assumed Xavier's place. "In this life, he detached and left."

She revealed she had suffered from post-partum depression after her first child, and had a psychotic break after the second child. She believes this was Vivienna's fate as well.

It has taken Angel a while to get her meds right, but added, "I feel I'm functional. There's a part of Xavier in me, too."

My Soul Writing

Angel chose to experience the emotions of Vivienna in this life so she would better understand—both on soul level and in the physical body—the emotional impact of depression. While she did not cause any physical harm to her family, she did harm them in terms of preventing them from experiencing a happy, loving and contented family life. Yet this was something they each agreed to--Xavier and the children—to deepen their understanding of living with someone incapable of emotionally expressing or attaching herself. Vivienna was trapped in that body—unable to acquire help because then help was not available. For Angel to reverse roles and take on that condition only deepens her soul's understanding of that element of emotional experience and growth. In so understanding, Angel has been able to get through her own issues in this life with grace, so that the karmic implications are not that great. Xavier felt some resentment and rightfully so—so in this life switched roles to counter the attitude he had toward his wife. This attitude was greater than revealed in the regression—so this is why it was repeated. It is being handled as best it can be and should be resolved so no further lifetimes will be impacted by it.

When asked several weeks later if she had experienced any new reveals since the session, Angel said she discovered that her ex-husband and sister-in-law in her present life mirrored some of the people in her regression. "Initially after the regression, I thought a lot about my ex-husband and sister-in-law and me in my present life—how they have excluded me from their lives," she said. "I would get attacks where I would feel deep pain that came from nowhere and then would go away. Nothing in particular triggered this pain. It would come out of nowhere and then disappear."

Angel had described a dull area around her heart. In the regression, Xavier lamented that he and Vivienna had no relationship and that he envied other married couples who seemed happy. I asked Angel if there was a correlation between Xavier's sentiment and what she felt today that would explain that "dull area around the heart."

"I felt 'broken hearted' that my two soul mates—my ex and my ex sister-in-law—had become emotionally detached in my past and present lives," she explained. "Vivienna was upset when her husband said he no longer loved her and emotionally detached from her."

Also in her body scan, Angel said she felt the need to yell but no voice was there. I suggested this must have been the way Xavier felt, but it could very easily have been the way Vivienna felt as well. I asked Angel to elaborate on how that felt to her in the here and now and how she related that sense of having no voice to her past-life experience.

"Again, I am unsure whether I was Vivienna or Xavier or both," she reiterated. "I experienced no voice—unable to verbalize upset and frustration—instead just emotionally detached by Xavier and Vivienna who had a harder time with acceptance of the present situation. Yelling out in frustration would only help Vivienna and not Xavier. He already had made up his mind about detaching whereas Vivienna was still coming to terms with acceptance of her situation."

Angel indicated in the questionnaire that after giving birth to her second child, she found herself in the bathroom of the ER where she regressed to a life in which she was concerned she would be burned at the stake for being a witch. Angel said hospital officials had to break down the bathroom door to turn off the water.

I suggested we could connect this in two ways. One, the fact that this happened after childbirth and Angel indicated that Vivienna's condition may have been post-partum depression. Second, the act of desperation Angel took may have reflected the way Xavier felt in his marriage to Vivienna. I asked if she could see any connection of the past-life experience with her current life.

"In this life, I experienced a post-partum depression with both of my children—the second one became a post-partum psychosis during which I experienced the Salem situation," she explained. "The marriage of Xavier to Vivienna also was reflected in my present-day marriage to my ex-husband; he became totally emotionally detached from me many years before I realized he had, resulting in acute pain when I realized that he no longer loved me."

We re-examined Angel's body scan for any clues to a past-life connection. When I mentioned the tingling at the bottom of her left foot and side of her right foot, she attributed that to feeling "ungrounded—not attached to the earth." She described her shoulder discomfort as being akin to carrying a heavy bag on her back. She felt this was tied to Xavier feeling a "heavy load on his back" and said she saw this both physically and metaphorically. The tightness in her lower jaw was attributed to Vivienna's inability to fully express feelings because she could not believe what was happening to her.

A theme in Xavier's life was his commitment to duty. He felt "kinda stuck" because he was responsible for the estate and apparently had a lot of people depending on him. I asked Angel if the phrase "kinda stuck" described her current life and she said it did. "I am 'kinda stuck' as far as my going forward with my divorce," she said. "I am "dragging my heels" and it is up to me to pursue the divorce."

In Angel's soul writing, she wrote: "Could see I am whole." I asked what that meant to her in terms of her past life and current condition.

"In my past and current lives, I have not felt whole due to my diagnosis of bipolar disease (this life) and post-partum and multiple depressions (both past and current lives)," she explained. "As I proceed with counseling and moving forward with a psychologically more healthy life in this life, I have feelings of happiness and am glad I am becoming more whole."

My soul writing suggested that Angel chose to experience the emotions of Vivienna's life in this life so she could better understand the emotional impact of depression and how it impacted her loved ones by preventing them from experiencing a happy, loving and contented family life. I sensed this was something her children agreed to in the pre-life planning session when they decided to incarnate again as Angel's sons. She believed it as well.

"I believe that my two sons chose this life before they were born in order to gain a fuller understanding of depression. Those who suffer from depression are unable to fully emotionally express or attach self," she explained. "As I have gotten healthier, I believe my children have increasingly attached themselves to me with the realization that I have been able to fully express and attach myself to them. I always have considered the role of mother to be very important. Even in my deepest depressed days, I made sure that they knew that I loved them deeply."

Although she had no prior knowledge about this past life, Angel said the regression clearly described this life's images and helped her to understand what both Xavier and Vivienna were feeling. Overall, our session had a positive impact on her life in terms of lessening the depression and becoming healthy both in awareness and acceptance of her life situation. While the condition did not go away completely, it subsided substantially.

Let Me Have Peace in My Life

Dr. Edith Fiore wrote: "My patients have been amazed to find that some recurring nightmares are actually flashbacks to experiences lived in previous lives." That was certainly the case with Irene, a 71-year old retired psychiatric nurse whose husband initially contacted me wondering if my program could be of help to her. He explained she had suffered from severe night terrors for many years, and no amount of counseling or psychiatric treatment had been of any use.

Irene described her night terrors as "vivid and very traumatic." They caused her heart rate to become elevated and since she was already in A-fib after chemotherapy, this was extremely dangerous. "They seem very real at the time and I remember them clearly the next day."

The nightmares took her to a concentration camp setting. They occurred regularly, with only a three or four night break between. In her nightmare, she was tortured, sexually abused, badly beaten, treated like a servant and saw babies and children being abused. The image would haunt her the next morning, so she had no relief.

Her body scan revealed discomfort in her stomach where she felt tight and bloated at her waist. One corner of her heart area hurt. She identified a large dark brown mark on her shoulder and another large brown mark over her left eye. "It just looks ugly," she said. "Spoils my looks. Won't wash off."

Irene regressed to what she believed to be the year 1921 in Bristol, England. There she saw herself as a 21-year-old woman named Mary George. She was slender and taller than she is now, with a pale complexion covered with excessive makeup. She had very short, bright red hair adorned with a band with black feathers. She had on "very pretty" black shoes with a strap. Her black dress had a hem of various lengths above her knee, with strips of shiny material with sequins or beads on the ends.

Mary described Bristol as a town consisting of old, narrow cobblestone streets. The identical houses were close together with no gaps between them. She was in a place identified by the word "BAR" on the window and there was music playing. It was located near the docks where the boats anchored and brought in goods.

Mary sat uncomfortably in an alcove at the back of the bar. She was hungry and was eating a tasteless mutton stew off a metal dish. She pulled a piece of bread from a loaf and dipped it in the gravy. She sipped bitter wine from a glass on the table. There were many people drinking at the bar, including other women who were dressed like her. The men wore white shirts and came from the better part of town. They looked and acted as if they were wealthy, buying drinks for everyone. Because of the proximity of the bar to the docks, sometimes the women would get gifts when the men came in off the boats.

Mary shared an upstairs room with five other women. "We have to entertain the clients, get them to buy a drink," she said. Some of the women were prostitutes. The younger ones had yet to enter into prostitution. Mary was one of them, managing to escape by being told to go upstairs and just "talk dirty" to the clients. She thought the fact that the owner liked her gave her special privileges. She set up clients for the other women to have sex with. The place was full of gaslights, big mirrors and was very smoky. She called it "a sleazy place." She did not like it much and felt used, but just tried to make a living.

The significant event in that life came much earlier when she was 8 years old. "I'm wearing rags," she said. "The house is dirty. A baby is crying somewhere. There are other children in this room." She identifies a younger brother and later says there are a total of three children. Her mother is there. "She's dressed, with a shawl around her shoulders. She looks so old. There's nothing on the floor—just floorboards. Everything is so dirty. I start to cry. My mother smacked me because I wet myself. It's not my fault. I didn't mean to do it." Irene starts to cry as this memory comes up.

The door slams and her father comes in from his job at the factory. He shouts at her mother, "Why isn't my damn supper ready?" Mary goes into the kitchen and hides behind the curtain under the sink. She says her father is always shouting at them. "He's always dirty," she says. "He smells. He doesn't wash very often. The baby is in the drawer crying. I go to him sometimes. I pick him up but he's all wet. He sometimes stops crying. She's [mom] got a pot of stew. She's putting up his supper for him. He's still very cross. I don't want him to see me. He wants a cup of tea. I can't see what's happening. I don't want to look. Nobody comes to find me. Nobody knows where I am.

"He's calling for me now. I haven't done anything wrong. I hope mother didn't tell him. 'Mary, I want to talk to you,' he says. I come out from the curtain. He'll get cross if I don't come. I stand by his side, look at his face and hope he's not cross with me. He wants me to go down to a shop for him to get a half-ounce of tobacco for his pipe. I said okay. He took the money out of his pocket. I had no coat. I went to the corner shop. It was so cold. I open the shop door. The bell clangs. I ask the lady for tobacco and I run back home because I was so cold. He seems a bit happier. He's stopped shouting. He's sitting in his chair by the fire. He lights his pipe. I hear Mother saying it's time for bed. I take my brother upstairs. We sleep in the same room. It's cold up there. I don't have a lot of clothes. There are no sheets on the bed, just an old blanket. I get my brother in bed. I hope and pray, 'Please don't let Daddy lose his temper tonight; don't let him shout tonight.' I am so tired. I want to go to sleep. Every night is the same. Dad just shouts, calls my mother all sorts of names and hits her. It was hard growing up. I wanted a lot of money and nice things and just get away from home. I wanted to be anywhere but home."

When she was 14, Mary's mother sold her to the man who ran the establishment where she was currently working. She never saw her family again. "I didn't know what happened there and what that place was," she said. "She just left me there with nothing but what I was wearing. I worked in the kitchen for a while making meals. The owner of the place would dress me up sometimes and just look at me. He put makeup all over my face. I didn't like the way I looked. He touched me and it didn't feel good. 'Don't touch me. Please don't do that. I don't like it,' I said. Then he'd shout at me to go back to the kitchen. 'You're only a little girl—go into the kitchen.' I tried to stay out of his way but it wasn't easy. I didn't like it there. I made up my mind I'd get a lot of money and live in a nice house where I wouldn't have to do anything. As I got older, I realized he must have liked me because I didn't have to do anything but sit with the clients."

When she turned 22, she had a birthday celebration with the other girls. That night the owner told her she had to start earning a living and to go upstairs and make some money. "I was waiting for that," she said. "If it meant going upstairs to earn money, I would do it so I could get out of there. It was difficult the first time. I didn't know what to do or how to do it. It hurt so much. I was so bruised, so rough. I kept thinking about the money and that it would be over soon. After a while it got easier. I kept saving money, hiding it under the floorboards when no one was looking. I just wanted to get out of this place."

At 36, she was told she was too old to work there and they didn't want her anymore. She had not saved enough to buy a house, but was able to secure lodging in a house where she paid rent for one room. Her life from this point on was simple. She did some shopping. She had a cat. She never went far from there. She did not work again.

Mary died at the age of 49. She was in a bed with an iron headboard in that same room. Her chest hurt and she could not breathe very well. She was alone. "I just feel so tired and worn out," she said. She began coughing up blood. "I just can't go on." Her last thoughts as her soul left her body were of relief. "It felt peaceful," she said. "I just felt so relieved I wasn't coughing anymore. I wanted a house so bad. I felt I deserved a house." She added that she does have a house in this life.

Similarities between that life and hers exist in the way she grew up, except her father wasn't like her previous father. Then, as in this life, she grew up poor and always wanted a house. "Growing up was very similar to Mary's life," Irene said. "My father was good with the children, but the poverty was the same. When I was 15, I left school. My mother got me a job in a doctor's house as a live-in servant. I hated the job—long hours and isolated. It was just the doctor and his wife in this huge house. I lived in the attic area. Just similar to Mary's life."

Irene's Soul Writing

Mary. I want a better life for myself. I hated my life. Will I ever have a house of my own? Please let me have peace in my life. I want my own clothes. Please make my life better. I want to be rich, not owned by anyone.

I asked whether the sentiments expressed in her soul writing were playing out in this life.

"I have been rich in the past, but learned money does not buy happiness," she replied. "I am not well off at the moment, but do have enough for my needs and have never been happier."

While Irene could not see many of the tie-ins between Mary's life and her own, she could identify with Mary being told at age 36 that she was too old to work anymore and was turned away.

"I excelled at my nursing job but was turned down for further training as an RN because I was 'too old' at 40," she said.

Interesting to note that despite the fact that Irene's night terrors had her in a Nazi concentration camp, her past-life journey took her elsewhere. In looking more closely at Mary's life, however, we see many of the same challenges present. She was malnourished; lived in a small, dirty sub-standard shelter; shared her blanket-less bed with other children; had little clothing to protect her from the elements; was beaten and sexually abused; and worked hard. While she may not have gotten the year right, or could not draw the parallels between that life and her present life, in the end it did not matter because the awareness alone made a strong impact on her life in that the night terrors ceased after our session.

Irene's journey is a good example of the healing nature of past-life work. A spontaneous healing is the highest attainment when dealing with karmic issues involving a chronic condition. Having Irene experience this fulfilled the project in a way I had not anticipated—and it makes for a good ending to this book!

Chapter Ten

Using Soul Writing For
Past Life Information

As a past-life therapist, I know the value of a private regression session in which the therapist and client can engage in a one-on-one conversation about specific events in that lifetime and then compare them with what is occurring in their present life. You can see in this book that the regression laid the groundwork by providing the participant with details about the lifetime that was most impacting their chronic condition today. The soul-writing session, added at the end of the regression, then built on what they experienced in the regression, giving them a fuller and clearer understanding of the origin of the karmic issues they were dealing with now. Since discovering the power of these two modalities working together, I give my clients the option of adding a soul-writing session at the end of each regression.

One thing I would like to make clear. Soul writing is NOT automatic writing. There is a difference between the two. Edgar

Cayce considered inspirational or soul writing as coming from the divine source within, and, as such, it is a means for soul development. Automatic writing, on the other hand, comes from an outside source, which is sometimes comprised of low influences. Other differences are as follows:

SOUL WRITING	AUTOMATIC WRITING
Includes meditation	No meditation
Total awareness	No awareness
Allow and consciously watch writing proceed.	No control of hand; happens by itself
Handwriting same	Handwriting different
Prayer of Protection	Prayer Omitted
Writing guides soul	Writing directs or impels

Now that you know the difference between the two, you may be asking yourself—well, what good does this do me if I don't know how to write in an altered state of consciousness? The answer is anyone can learn how to do soul writing. Most get something on their first try—whether it's a word, a phrase or a full sentence. With practice, nearly everyone succeeds.

While there are only four main steps to doing soul writing: meditation, white light prayer for protection, asking the question; waiting for and then receiving the answer on paper, the following will give you an outline of other useful steps to help you get started.

1. Find a Sacred Place

Quiet, privacy, soft lighting and a comfortable place to sit are the primary requirements for successful soul writing. Locate that special place in your home for you to connect with spirit— a place where you feel peaceful and centered. Eventually you'll be able to write anywhere.

2. Set the Stage

Now that you have the right space, surround yourself with items that enhance your spiritual connection and enable you to go into a deeper state of meditation. Music, candles, chimes, incense, totems, and other tools lift you higher as you communicate with spirit.

3. Same Time, Same Place

Whether it's first thing in the morning, mid-day or before bed, one of the most compelling reasons to write at the same time each day is that it establishes a pattern and becomes a natural part of your routine. With our busy schedules, this is not always possible. As beginners, however, it would be helpful if you made an appointment with spirit to write at the same time every day. Once you become more experienced, you'll find that when you are in need of guidance, you can stop what you are doing, take a few cleansing breaths, do a brief meditation, say a prayer of protection, and seek guidance on whatever issue is before you.

4. Pen Versus Keyboard

Writing with a pencil, a pen or on a keyboard is a matter of personal preference. Certainly you are as guided at the computer as you are with pen in hand. However, writing by hand has a different feel to it than composing on a keyboard; you sense a spiritual presence within, gently guiding your hand. When you sit at a computer and poise your hands over a keyboard, some part of you must remain in a conscious state in order to remember the location of the appropriate keys. One key off and you won't be able to read the message. Having to consistently check the placement of your fingers on the keyboard can disrupt the flow of the message, because it pulls you in and out of your meditative state. To find out which works best for you, experiment with the pen or pencil over a period of a few days and then switch to the keyboard to record your messages electronically over a similar length of time. Afterwards, decide which method you prefer and commit to that.

5. Focus on an Ideal

An ideal is defined as something beyond and above us toward which we build. It's a guiding pattern in your life—the "why" of why you do the things you do and say the things you say. Often it is the expression of a person's mission in life, i.e. to be a catalyst for change; to be a truth seeker; to attract prosperity; to manifest love. Before you begin your writing session, formulate your ideal in your mind, write it down, focus on it and repeat it as a silent mantra. Then step aside and allow the response to flow in accordance with that ideal.

6. Meditation is Key

Soul writing is a written form of meditation. Closing your eyes, learning to quiet your mind, relaxing every part of your body through deep breathing, ignoring distractions and going into a peaceful, centered place is an essential part of the process. Music or nature sounds in the background are helpful tools to reach this blissful state. There are many guided meditations available if you prefer to have someone lead you into this relaxed state, but the goal is to learn to do this on your own.

7. Say a Prayer of Protection

Saying a prayer and asking for protection before working with spirit is an imperative part of the process and everyone should do it—whether you are a novice or an experienced metaphysician. Asking for white light protection ensures that you are sealed in an impenetrable bubble, strengthens your aura, and wards off any dark energy.

8. Get Ready to Write

Patience and trusting your source is essential. Soul writing is a spontaneous process. For it to succeed you have to get out of the way. If you try to manipulate or force the words, you will disrupt the process. Write (or in your mind state) the intent for the session. Open your eyes halfway so you can see the paper or screen in front of you. Hold the pen or pencil loosely in your hand. If you are working on a keyboard, poise your fingers above the keys and wait.

9. Allow the Message to Proceed

Getting started is always the most difficult part of the process. Impatience sets in and we give up. If you are writing by hand, you can jumpstart the process by drawing ovals or continuous loops. Eventually the words will flow out of those doodles. Those new to the process may only get a few scribbles on the page. Don't get discouraged—just go with the flow. The words will come in their own time. They also will stop in their own time. Soul writing can feel like a form of rapid dictation so write it as it comes. If no words come but a thought enters your mind, write that down and go back to the ovals. Do not let your internal editor complain about how the writing looks, how a word is spelled, or that the punctuation or grammar is incorrect.

True soul writing is never critical or negative. It does not challenge or bully you into a change of attitude nor tell you what to do. Instead, it gently offers guidance on options to consider. It does not use foul language. If it does, you need to stop immediately. Go back, say the prayer of protection again and reinforce your white light protection. Remember that soul writing comes from a very high level. Your loving Source would never call you names or make demands.

Write down whatever you receive. Don't question it (unless it absolutely does not feel right) and don't shut down and refuse to hear the message. Remain open and receptive. Remember, you are asking for divine guidance. You may not always like what you hear, but if you proceed with an open heart, you will embrace the results.

You will find most soul writing includes the word "we" rather than "I." The latter is more ego-based and indicative of automatic writing. The use of the word "we" lifts you higher into the collective consciousness. It reinforces a sense that you are never alone; that you are part of the collective universe, in balance and harmony with the All That Is.

10. Wait Before You Read

Often when you put the writing away and go back to it a few days, weeks, or months later, it has a totally new meaning. When you do read the message, do so from your spiritual self. Take a moment to reflect on the message and see if it resonates with you on any level. Guidance from your higher self is not intended to be a roadmap to tell you which way to go. Instead its purpose is to offer you a new perspective so that you can begin to see things differently.

11. Keep Your Writing Safe

Safeguard your writings from prying eyes. Remember, deep soul writing is a conversation with your higher self, your guides, your Source, or your angel—with emphasis on the word *your*. If you are working out issues that happened in a past life, it may appear to the casual reader that you are writing about yourself in the here and now. Your "what ifs" may be your way of exploring various options about that life, but the reader may think you are recording an actual event in this life. You can imagine where this could lead.

12. A Few Final Dos and Don'ts

Soul writing is a tool of transformation. Be prepared for your life to change once you begin writing on a regular basis.

Do not try soul writing when you are under the influence of anything like drugs, tobacco, alcohol, junk food, etc. that may cause your system to slow down or speed up. These factors may lower your vibrational rate and that will lessen the productivity of the session.

It's not unusual to feel tired after a writing session, especially when you are new to the process. This usually lessens the more you write as you become accustomed to operating in an altered state for longer periods of time.

If you do not know what to ask, seek a message about something that is impacting you today. You may want to know about the source of your talents and abilities just as much as your challenges in this life.

Watch for synchronicities and messages that will begin to appear after you start writing. They may appear in music, in a book, a television program, in a movie, or through a casual comment.

Always say thank you!

It is not necessary to master all of these steps to do soul writing, but it is worth noting that incorporating each of these practices is helpful in achieving a deeper level of writing. Once you do some of them—like finding your sacred space— you won't have to do them again. Of all these steps, the most important ones can be completed in a matter of minutes.

- Enter an altered state of consciousness through meditation (deep breathing, relaxation exercises).
- Surround yourself with white light and say a prayer of protection.
- Ask your question.
- Wait for the answer and then commit it to paper.

Soul writing can be applied to many areas of your life. Past-life exploration is just one of them. To find out about the others and to get a more detailed description of the soul-writing process, you may want to read my book, *Soul Writing: Conversing With Your Higher Self* (print or Kindle version available on Amazon). Examples of others who have used soul writing to access past-life information can be found in my second book: *Your Soul Remembers: Accessing Your Past Lives Through Soul Writing.* Information on both can be found at www.joannedimaggio.com.

References

Cayce, Edgar. Edgar Cayce Readings. Virginia Beach, VA: Edgar Cayce Foundation

Cranston, Sylvia & Williams, Carey. *Reincarnation, A New Horizon in Science, Religion and Society.* New York, NY: Julian Press, 1984.

Fiore, Dr. Edith. *You Have Been Here Before. A Psychologist Looks at Past Lives.* New York, NY: Ballantine Books, 1978.

Newton, Michael, Ph.D. *Journey of Souls, Case Studies of Life Between Life.* St. Paul, MN: Llewellyn Publications, 1996.

Oppenheim, Garrett. "A Karmic Case of Polio." *Venture Inward*, p. 33. (November/December, 1989).

Reilly, Harold J., "Healing Begins in the Mind," *The Searchlight*, p. 5. (February, 1960).

Schwimmer, George. "Inner Healing from Past Lives." *Venture Inward*, pp. 12, 51. (September/October, 2004).

Stevenson, Dr. Ian. "Birthmarks and Birth Defects Corresponding to Wounds on Deceased Persons." *Journal of Scientific Exploration*, Vol. 7, No. 4, pp. 403-410, 1993.

Talbot, Michael. *Your Past Lives. A Reincarnation Handbook.* New York, NY: Harmony Books, 1987.

Todeschi, Kevin J. & Reed, Henry, Ph.D. "Karma as Memory." *Venture Inward*, p. 41. (April-June, 2013).

Unterberger, Gregg. "Healing Effects of Past Life Regression." *Venture Inward*, p. 23. (April-June, 2010).

Weiss, Brian L., M.D. *Through Time Into Healing.* New York, NY: Simon & Schuster, 1992.

Williston, Glenn & Johnstone, Judith. *Discovering Your Past Lives. Spiritual Growth through a Knowledge of Past Lifetimes.* Wellingborough, Northamptonshire, England: Aquarian Press, 1983.

Woodward, Mary Anne. *Scars of the Soul: Holistic Healing in the Edgar Cayce Readings*. Fair Grove, MO: Brindabella Books, 1985.

Woolger, Roger, Ph.D. "A Rebuttal to Ian Stevenson." *Venture Inward*, p. 34. November/December, 1989).

Woolger, Roger, Ph.D. *Healing Your Past Lives, Exploring the Many Lives of the Soul.* Boulder, CO: Sounds True, 2004.

Woolger, Roger, Ph.D. *Other Lives, Other Selves: A Jungian Psychologist Discovers Past Lives.* New York, NY: Doubleday, 1988.

About the Author

JOANNE DIMAGGIO, MA, CHT, is an inspired teacher who has been professionally pursuing past-life research and therapy for over twenty-five years. She headed her own past-life research center outside of Chicago and brought that to Virginia in 1995. Joanne earned her Master's in Transpersonal Studies degree and her Spiritual Mentor certification through Atlantic University. Her thesis, on inspirational writing, served as the basis of her first book, *Soul Writing: Conversing With Your Higher Self.* Her last book was *Your Soul Remembers: Accessing Your Past Lives through Soul Writing.* Joanne continues to lecture and conduct workshops on soul writing across the country, sharing her knowledge through blogs, online courses, magazine articles, and radio programs.

Related Titles

If you enjoyed *Karma Can Be a Real Pain,* you may also enjoy other Rainbow Ridge titles. Read more about them at *www.rainbowridgebooks.com.*

*Your Soul Remembers: Accessing Your
Past Lives through Soul Writing*
by Joanne DiMaggio

God's Message to the World: You've Got Me All Wrong
by Neale Donald Walsch

The Secret of Effortless Being
by Ronny Hatchwell and Zach Sivan

Rita's World
by Frank DeMarco

Soul Courage
by Tara-jenelle Walsch

Quantum Economics
by Amit Goswami

Coming Full Circle: Ancient Teachings for a Modern World
by Lynn Andrews

Consciousness: Bridging the Gap Between Conventional Science and the New Super Science of Quantum Mechanics
by Eva Herr

Messiah's Handbook: Reminders for the Advanced Soul
by Richard Bach

Blue Sky, White Clouds
by Eliezer Sobel

Inner Vegas: Creating Miracles, Abundance, and Health
by Joe Gallenberger

When the Horses Whisper: The Wisdom of Wise and Sentient Beings
by Rosalyn W. Berne, Ph.D.

Lessons in Courage
by Bonnie Glass-Coffin and don Oscar Miro-Quesada

The Healing Curve
by Sara Chetkin

God Within
by Patti Conklin

Conversations with God for Parents
by Neale Donald Walsch, with
Laurie Farley and Emily Filmore

Dance of the Electric Hummingbird
by Patricia Walker

Rainbow Ridge Books publishes spiritual, metaphysical,
and self-help titles, and is distributed by Square One
Publishers in Garden City Park, New York.

To contact authors and editors, peruse our titles, and
see submission guidelines, please visit our website at
www.rainbowridgebooks.com.

For orders and catalogs, please call toll-free:
(877) 900-BOOK.